Dynamics of World Revolution Today

Dynamics of World Revolution Today

WITHDRAWN
- ☐ DESELECTED
- ☐ LOST
- ☐ DAMAGED
- ☐ MISSING (INV.)
- ☐ OTHER_____

PATHFINDER PRESS

NEW YORK

Edited by Will Reissner
First Edition, 1974
Copyright©1974 by Pathfinder Press
All Rights Reserved
Library of Congress Catalog Card Number 74-15528
ISBN 87348-374-x (cloth), 87348-400-2 (paper)

Manufactured in the United States of America

Pathfinder Press, Inc.
410 West Street
New York, N.Y. 10014

Contents

Preface   9

For Early Reunification of the World Trotskyist
Movement   13

Dynamics of World Revolution Today   25

The Unfolding New World Situation
        by Jack Barnes   75

The World Political Situation and the Immediate
Tasks of the Fourth International
    I. Chief Features of the World Political
        Situation   111
   II. The World Revolution Resumes Its Main
        Course   119
  III. Radicalization and Mobilization of the
        Allies of the Proletariat   136
   IV. Mobilization of the Counterrevolution
        and the Struggle Against It   152
    V. Maturing of the Subjective Conditions
        for Revolution   176

Preface

The four documents in this compilation will be of interest primarily to socialists. However, a broader audience of those concerned about the increasingly acute crises of capitalism and aware of the deepening trend of society on a world scale toward a higher form of economy will find the Trotskyist viewpoint presented here worthy of attention.

The basic assumption in all four documents is that capitalism has long ago overridden all national boundaries economically in the search for areas of investment, sources of raw materials, exploitation of cheap labor power, and the extraction of profits.

Because of their global economic and political interests, the ruling classes of the advanced capitalist countries have a piratical interest in developments on all continents. And they are ready to intervene in the most forceful way both politically and economically when they consider that their interests require it. The intervention of the Kennedy, Johnson, and Nixon administrations in Indochina at the risk of touching off a third world war provides a prime example of the foreign policy that results from the needs of an imperialist power like the United States.

The imperialist statesmen, while always giving top priority to their own national interests, also bear in mind the needs of the capitalist system as a whole in its conflict with the global trend toward a new social system based on fulfilling human needs rather than subordinating those needs to the imperatives of profit-making.

In a parallel way, as representatives of the long-range interests of the international working class and its allies, socialists base themselves on a realistic appraisal of the situation in the world. In accordance with the particular

9

configurations of this situation, they determine the strategy and tactics applicable in their own countries.

Further in this pattern of thought, revolutionists who are serious about overturning the capitalist system take an international approach in devising the means to achieve this goal. The means is a mass revolutionary party. The Bolshevik party constructed by Lenin and his team still stands as a model in this respect. Such parties cannot be built without international cooperation among the cadres of revolutionary socialism. When Leon Trotsky founded the Fourth International in 1938, one of his principal aims was to help assure continuation of the Leninist tradition of party building in both program and practice.

The four documents in this volume deal with long-range questions. Conjunctural situations, while referred to in passing, have been subordinated to analysis of trends and problems stretching over decades. The long-range view provides the common framework.

The first document, "For Early Reunification of the World Trotskyist Movement," is important as a condensed statement of the program of the world Trotskyist movement. It was drawn up in March 1963 by the Political Committee of the Socialist Workers Party, the American Trotskyist organization, when it became clear that it was possible to heal a ten-year split in the Fourth International on a principled basis. This document, the earliest of the four in this collection, pointed out sixteen areas of agreement in the world movement and concluded that "in view of the agreement on these basic positions, the world Trotskyist movement is duty bound to press for reunification."

The resolution was adopted by the two factions that had been involved in the split and became the statement of principles upon which the Fourth International reunited at a world congress held in June 1963.

In commenting on the reunification in the fall 1963 issue of the *International Socialist Review,* Farrell Dobbs and Joseph Hansen, two leading figures of the Socialist Workers Party and of the world Trotskyist movement, hailed the closing of ranks on a principled program and pointed out that now "united forces could be brought to bear in the promising situations developing in all directions."

The second document in this compilation, "The Dynamics of World Revolution Today," was one of the key resolutions adopted at the 1963 reunification congress of the Fourth International. It is of special interest because of its careful analysis of the three sectors of the world revolution and their interaction—the proletarian revolution in the advanced capitalist countries, the colonial revolution in the so-called third world, and the political revolution in the Soviet Union and other workers states. The resolution develops in an extended way an analysis entitled "The World Struggle for Socialism" adopted at the June 1961 convention of the Socialist Workers Party.

The third document, "The Unfolding New World Situation," is based on a report given by Jack Barnes, national secretary of the Socialist Workers Party, at a meeting of the National Committee of the SWP in April 1973. This document brings in recent developments, particularly the detente between Washington and Moscow and Peking, and assesses their meaning for the revolutionary-socialist movement.

The final document, "The World Political Situation and the Immediate Tasks of the Fourth International," which was submitted in January 1974 for discussion in the world Trotskyist movement, is of importance because of its restatement of the aims of the Fourth International set forth by Leon Trotsky in 1938 and its assessment of where the Fourth International stands today in the difficult work of building mass revolutionary parties. The document deals with the current world situation in the light of the prognosis made by Trotsky but stresses the party-building problem.

The frank statement of the difficulties facing small groups that have taken as their aim nothing less than toppling the capitalist system should help underline the suggestions in the document as to how to overcome these difficulties. While the document was written for the consideration of the cadres of the world Trotskyist movement, other tendencies may want to weigh its applicability to their own situation.

THE EDITOR
AUGUST 1974

FOR EARLY REUNIFICATION OF THE WORLD TROTSKYIST MOVEMENT

The world Trotskyist movement has been split since 1954. Various efforts in the past to heal the rupture proved unsuccessful. On both sides, however, it has been felt for some time that a new and more vigorous effort for reunification should be made in view of the encouraging opportunities that now exist to further the growth and influence of the Fourth International, the World Party of Socialist Revolution.

The Socialist Workers Party has stressed that a principled basis exists for uniting the main currents of the world Trotskyist movement. During the past year the International Secretariat took the initiative in urging the necessity and practicality of ending the split. For its side the International Committee proposed that a Parity Committee be set up. Although some of the comrades in the IC viewed this as involving no more than a practical step to facilitate common discussion and united work in areas of mutual interest, the majority, it appears clear, welcomed the formation of the committee as an important step toward early reunification.

While substantial differences still remain, especially over the causes of the 1954 split, the area of disagreement appears of secondary importance in view of the common basic program and common analysis of major current events in world developments which unite the two sides. With good will it should be possible to contain the rec-

13

ognized remaining differences within a united organization, subject to further discussion and clarification, thus making possible the great advantages that would come through combining the forces, skills, and resources of all those now adhering to one side or the other.

The main fact is that the majority on both sides are now in solid agreement on the fundamental positions of the world Trotskyist movement. As briefly as possible we will indicate the points of common outlook:

1. The present agonizing world crisis reflects at bottom a prolonged crisis in revolutionary leadership. The development of the productive forces on a global scale has made the world overripe for socialism. Only a socialist planned world economy can rapidly overcome the economic underdevelopment of the colonial and semicolonial countries, deliver mankind from the threat of nuclear extinction, and assure a world society of enduring peace, of boundless plenty, the unlimited expansion of culture and the achievement of full freedom for all. Without the international victory of socialism, decaying capitalism will continue to waste enormous resources, to hold two-thirds of the earth's population in abject poverty, to maintain social and racial inequality, and to support dictatorial regimes. To complete this grim perspective of hunger, insecurity, inequality and oppressive rule, capitalism offers the permanent threat of nuclear destruction.

2. The delay of the world socialist revolution beyond the expectations of all the great Marxists before our time is due basically to the lack of capacity of the traditional leaderships of the working-class movement and to their cynical service as labor lieutenants of the capitalist class or the Kremlin bureaucracy. They are responsible for preventing the main revolutionary postwar crises of 1918-23 and of 1943-47, as well as the lesser crisis of 1932-37, from ending as they should have ended with the proletariat coming to power in the advanced capitalist countries.

3. Only by building new revolutionary Marxist mass parties capable of leading the working class and working farmers to power can the world crisis be met successfully and a third world war prevented. To build such parties

is the aim and purpose of the world Trotskyist movement. A program of transitional slogans and measures plays a key role in party-building work inasmuch as the principal problem in overcoming the crisis of leadership is to bridge the gap between the present consciousness of the masses — which is centered around immediate problems and preoccupations — and the level of consciousness required to meet the objective necessity of overthrowing capitalism and building workers states based upon democratically elected and democratically functioning councils of the working people. Leninist methods must be used to construct revolutionary-socialist parties. These include patient, persistent recruitment of workers to the nuclei of revolutionary-socialist parties already established; but also, where necessity or opportunity dictates, flexible advances toward various tendencies in mass organizations which may eventually be brought to the program of revolutionary Marxism. Individual recruitment and tactical moves of wide scope are complementary ways of party construction, but each carries its own problems and special dangers. In the one instance a tendency toward sectarianism can arise out of converting enforced isolation into a virtue; in the other, adaptation to a reformist environment can lead to rightist opportunism. In the tactic known as "entryism," where unusually difficult and complicated situations can occur, it should be the norm for those engaging in it to maintain a sector of open public work, including their own Trotskyist publication. Departure from this norm must be weighed with full consciousness of the heavy risks involved.

4. The Fourth International as an international organization, and its sections as national parties, must adhere to the principles of democratic centralism. Both theory and historic experience have demonstrated the correctness of these principles. Democratic centralism corresponds to the need for quick, disciplined action in meeting revolutionary tasks while at the same time assuring the freedom of discussion and the right to form tendencies without which genuine political life is denied to the ranks. In its adherence to internal democracy, the world Trotskyist movement stands at the opposite pole from the stifling regimes imposed on working-class organizations controlled by

bureaucrats trained in the schools of Stalinism, the Social Democracy or reformist unionism.

5. The bureaucratic reformist and Stalinist machines do not use the organized strength of the working class to overthrow capitalism where this is possible. They are primarily interested in their own privileges and power instead of the long-range interests of the working class. Because of inertia. an antisocialist outlook, or recognition that an upsurge can sweep over their heads, they undertake struggles in the interests of the proletariat only with great reluctance and under great pressure. While condemning and opposing the twin evils of reformism and Stalinism, Trotskyists refuse to identify the genuinely socialist or Communist workers of these mass organizations with their treacherous leaderships. The Trotskyist movement recognizes that the main task is not simply to wage literary war on reformism and Stalinism, but to actually win these socialist- and communist-minded workers to the program and organization of revolutionary Marxism. Under the pressure of long years of prosperity in the advanced capitalist countries and in reaction to the crimes of Stalinism, petty-bourgeois intellectuals have opened a wide assault on the fundamentals of Marxism. It is necessary to wage a firm ideological struggle against this revisionist current.

6. The Soviet Union is still a workers state despite the usurpation of power by a privileged bureaucracy. The mode of production is noncapitalist, having emerged from the destruction of capitalism by the socialist October Revolution; and, whatever its deficiencies, lapses and even evils, it is progressive compared to capitalism. The tremendous expansion of Soviet productive forces through a colossal industrial and cultural revolution transformed a backward peasant country into the second industrial power of the world, actually challenging imperialism's lead in many fields of technology. This great new fact of world history bears witness to the mighty force inherent in planned economy and demonstrates the correctness of the Trotskyist position of unconditional defense of the degenerated workers state against imperialism.

7. In the wake of World War II, the Soviet bureaucracy was able to extend its power and its parasitism into the

so-called "people's democracies" of Eastern Europe and North Korea. But to maintain its position of special privilege, it had to destroy capitalism in these countries, doing so by bureaucratic-military means. That such means could succeed was due to the abnormal circumstances of temporary collapse of the local capitalist-landlord rule coupled with extreme weakness of the working class following the carnage of war and occupation. In this way deformed workers states came into existence. These are defended by the Trotskyist movement against imperialist attempts to reintroduce capitalism.

8. In the workers states where proletarian democracy was smashed by Stalinism, or where it never came into existence because of Stalinist influence, it is necessary to struggle for its restoration or construction, for democratic administration of the state and of the planned economy by the toiling masses. Through a political counterrevolution, Stalin destroyed the proletarian democracy of the time of Lenin and Trotsky. The Leninist forces are therefore faced with the need to organize revolutionary Marxist parties to provide leadership for the working class in exercising its right to overthrow the dictatorial rule of the bureaucratic caste and to replace it with forms of proletarian democracy. This signifies a political revolution. With the rebirth of proletarian democracy on a higher level, the workers states — the Soviet Union above all — will regain the attractive power enjoyed before the days of Stalin, and this will give fresh impetus to the struggle for socialism in the advanced capitalist countries.

9. The appearance of a workers state in Cuba — the exact form of which is yet to be settled — is of special interest since the revolution there was carried out under a leadership completely independent from the school of Stalinism. In its evolution toward revolutionary Marxism, the July 26 Movement set a pattern that now stands as an example for a number of other countries.

10. As a result of the new upsurge of the world revolution, above all the tremendous victory in China which changed the relationship of class forces on an international scale, the Soviet proletariat — already strengthened and made self-confident through the victory over German imperialism in World War II and the great economic,

technological and cultural progress of the Soviet Union — has exerted increasingly strong pressure on the bureaucratic dictatorship, especially since Stalin's death. In hope of easing this pressure, the ruling caste has granted concessions of considerable scope, abolishing the extreme forms of police dictatorship (dissolution of the forced labor camps and modification of Stalin's brutal labor code, destroying the cult of Stalin, rehabilitating many victims of Stalin's purges, granting a significant rise in the standard of living of the people, even easing the strictures against freedom of thought and discussion in various fields). The Khrushchev regime has no intention of dismantling the bureaucratic dictatorship a piece at a time; its aim is not "self-reform" but maintenance of the rule of the caste in face of mounting popular pressures. But the masses accept the concessions as partial payment on what is due and seek to convert the gains into new points of support in pressing for the ultimate objective of restoring democratic proletarian controls over the economy and the state. This slow but solid strengthening of the position of the proletariat in the European workers states is one of the basic causes of the world crisis of Stalinism.

11. The differences which finally shattered the monolithic structure of Stalinism began in a spectacular way with ideological and political conflict between the Yugoslav and Soviet Communist party leaderships. This conflict was widened by the attempted political revolution undertaken by the Hungarian workers. The Cuban Revolution deepened the crisis still further. With the Chinese-Soviet rift it has become one of the most important questions of world politics. While expressing in an immediate sense the conflict of interests among the various national bureaucratic groups, and between the Soviet bureaucracy and the working classes of countries under its influence, the crisis reflects fundamentally the incompatibility of Stalinism with living victorious revolutions in which the militant vanguard seeks a return to the doctrines of Lenin. The crisis is thus highly progressive in character, marking an important stage in the rebuilding of a revolutionary Marxist world mass movement.

12. In conjunction with the world crisis of Stalinism, the colonial revolution is now playing a key role in the world

revolutionary process. Within little more than a decade, it has forced imperialism to abolish direct colonial rule almost completely and to turn to indirect rule as a substitute; i.e., form a new "partnership" with the colonial bourgeoisie, even though this bourgeoisie in some places may be only embryonic. But this attempt to prevent the countries awakened by the colonial revolution from breaking out of the world capitalist system runs into an insuperable obstacle. It is impossible in these countries to solve the historic problems of social, economic, and cultural liberation and development without overthrowing capitalism as well as breaking the grip of imperialism. The colonial revolution therefore tends to flow into the channel of permanent revolution, beginning with. a radical agrarian reform and heading toward the expropriation of imperialist holdings and "national" capitalist property, the establishment of a workers state and a planned economy.

13. Along the road of a revolution beginning with simple democratic demands and ending in the rupture of capitalist property relations, guerrilla warfare conducted by landless peasant and semiproletarian forces, under a leadership that becomes committed to carrying the revolution through to a conclusion, can play a decisive role in undermining and precipitating the downfall of a colonial or semicolonial power. This is one of the main lessons to be drawn from experience since the Second World War. It must be consciously incorporated into the strategy of building revolutionary Marxist parties in colonial countries.

14. Capitalism succeeded in winning temporary stability again in Western Europe after the Second World War. This setback for the working class was due primarily to the treacherous role played by the Stalinist and Social-Democratic leaderships, which prevented the masses from taking the road of socialist revolution during the big postwar revolutionary crisis. However, this temporary stabilization of capitalism and the subsequent upsurge of productive forces gave rise to more extensive, and ultimately more explosive, contradictions. These involve the other imperialist powers, above all the USA and Japan. They include sharpening competition in a geographically contracting world market; increasing incompatibility between the need to fight inflation and the need to transform

potential major economic crises into more limited recessions; mounting conflict between the desirability of maintaining "social peace" and the necessity to attack the workers' standard of living, job conditions, and employment opportunities in order to strengthen competitive efficiency. These contradictions point to increasingly fierce class battles which could become lifted from the economic to the political level in acute form and, under favorable conditions of leadership, arouse the labor movement to a new upsurge in the imperialist countries, challenging capitalism in its last citadels.

15. Socialist victory in the advanced capitalist countries constitutes the only certain guarantee of enduring peace. Since the close of World War II, imperialism has methodically prepared for another conflict, one in which the capitalist world as a whole would be mobilized against the workers states, with the Soviet Union as the main target. Rearmament has become the principal permanent prop of capitalist economy today, an economic necessity that dovetails with the political aims of the American capitalist class at the head of the world alliance of capitalism. American imperialism has stationed counterrevolutionary forces in a vast perimeter around China and the Soviet Union. Its first reaction to new liberating struggles is to seek to drown them in blood. Its armed interventions have become increasingly dangerous. In the crisis over Cuba's efforts to strengthen its military defense, the billionaire capitalist families who rule America demonstrated that they were prepared to launch a nuclear attack against the Soviet Union and even risk the very existence of civilization and of mankind. This unimaginable destructive power can be torn from the madmen of Wall Street only by the American working class. The European socialist revolution will play a decisive role in helping to bring the American proletariat up to the level of the great historic task which it faces — responsibility for the final and decisive victory of world socialism.

16. While participating wholeheartedly in all popular mass movements for unilateral nuclear disarmament, while fighting for an immediate end to all nuclear tests, the world Trotskyist movement everywhere clearly emphasizes the fundamental dilemma facing humanity: world socialism or

nuclear annihilation. A clear understanding of this dilemma does not demoralize the masses. On the contrary, it constitutes the strongest incentive to end capitalism and build socialism. It is a suicidal illusion to believe that peace can be assured through "peaceful coexistence" without ending capitalism. Above all in America. The best way to fight against the threat of nuclear war is to fight for socialism through class-struggle means.

In view of the agreement on these basic positions, the world Trotskyist movement is duty bound to press for reunification. It is unprincipled to seek to maintain the split. Reunification has also become an urgent practical question. On all sides, opportunities for growth are opening up for the revolutionary movement. The Cuban Revolution dealt a blow to the class-collaborationist policy of Stalinism in Latin America and other colonial countries. New currents, developing under the influence of the victory in Cuba, are groping their way to revolutionary socialism and seeking to apply the main lessons of the colonial revolution to their own situation. The Algerian Revolution has had a similar effect on the vanguard of the African revolutionary nationalist movement. To meet these leftward-moving currents, to work with them, even to combine with them without giving up any principles, has become an imperious necessity. Reunification will greatly facilitate success in this task by strengthening our own forces and bringing the attractiveness of Trotskyism into sharp organizational focus. The immediate corollaries will be increased effectiveness of our defense of the colonial revolutions within the imperialist countries and the added weight which the principled program of Trotskyism will gain among all serious revolutionists who seek the fundamental economic, social and political transformation of their countries. On the other hand, it is self-evident that the continued division of the world Trotskyist movement in factions wrangling over obscure issues will vitiate its capacity to attract these new forces on a considerable scale.

Similarly, the crisis of Stalinism, which has led to the great differentiation visible in the Chinese-Soviet rift, has unlocked tremendous forces within the Communist parties throughout the world. Attracted by our Leninist program and traditions, by the vindication of our decades of struggle against Stalinism, and by our insistence on internal democracy, many militants are puzzled and repelled by our lack of unity, by our seeming incapacity to mobilize our forces into a single cohesive organization. The reunification of the world Trotskyist movement would contribute powerfully towards reeducating Communist militants in the genuine spirit of Leninism, its real tradition of international solidarity and proletarian democracy. Obviously a united world Trotskyist movement would prove much more attractive to all those forces within the world Communist movement who are increasingly critical of Stalinism and its offshoots, and who are ready to examine the views of a movement which appears serious not only in its theory but in its organizational capacity.

Finally, we should consider with utmost attentiveness the problem of appealing to the youth, both workers and students, who are playing an increasingly decisive role in demonstrations, uprisings, and the leadership of revolutionary upheavals. The Cuban Revolution was essentially fought by the youth. Similar young people overthrew the corrupt dictatorial regimes of Menderes in Turkey and Syngman Rhee in South Korea. In the struggle for Negro equality in the USA, for solidarity with the Algerian Revolution in France, against rearmament in Japan and Western Germany and against unemployment in Britain, the shock forces are provided by the youth. Youth stand in the forefront of the fight to deepen and extend de-Stalinization in the USSR and the East European workers states. Throughout the world they are the banner bearers of the struggles for unilateral nuclear disarmament. We can attract the best layers of this new generation of rebels by our bold program, our fighting spirit and militant activity; we can only repel them by refusing to close ranks because of differences over past disputes of little interest to young revolutionists of action, who are primarily concerned about the great political issues and burning problems of today.

Early reunification, in short, has become a necessity for the world Trotskyist movement. Naturally, difficult problems will remain in various countries where the faction fight has been long and bitter. But these problems, too, can best be worked out under the conditions of general international reunification, so that it is possible for the outstanding leaders of both sides to begin the job of establishing a new comradely atmosphere and of removing fears which have no real basis in the situation in the world Trotskyist movement today. After a period of common fraternal activity in an increasing number of areas, we are convinced that what may appear at the outset to be insuperable local problems will be solved by the comrades themselves through democratic means.

We think that it should also be possible for a reunified organization to bring in recommendations for subsequent consideration and adoption which, without breaching the centralist side of democratic centralism, would remove any doubts that might still remain as to the guarantee of democratic rights contained in the statutes.

Our movement is faced with a responsibility as great and grave as the one it faced at the founding of the Fourth International in 1938. We ask both sides to decide at their international gatherings in the next months that the time has come to reunify the world Trotskyist movement, and that they will do this at a World Congress of Reunification to be held as rapidly as possible after these gatherings.

March 1, 1963

DYNAMICS OF
WORLD REVOLUTION TODAY

1. The General Background

The classical schema of world revolution assumed that the victory of socialism would occur first in the most industrially developed countries, setting an example for the less developed. "The more advanced countries show the more backward ones their own future," wrote Marx. For the victory of socialism, Marxism generally held that a highly developed industrial base and powerful proletariat as well as a strong and politically conscious labor movement were indispensable objective and subjective preconditions which could appear only with the full development of capitalism.

It is true that after the revolution of 1848, Marx voiced some misgivings about one of the political assumptions underlying this schema; namely, the capacity of the bourgeoisie to carry out a classical bourgeois-democratic revolution in countries where capitalism is still immature but where a modern proletariat already exists. Later Engels further undermined this schema when he pointed out that the relative weakness of political consciousness among the British working class was due precisely to the fact that Britain was the most advanced capitalist country, holding a world monopoly on high productivity.

At the beginning of the twentieth century, Trotsky, in 1905, in his theory of permanent revolution, which held that the working class would find itself compelled to carry out tasks historically belonging to the bourgeoisie, and

25

Lenin, in 1914, in his theory of imperialism, which included the view that the imperialist chain would break first at its weakest link, showed that they had come to understand the main consequence of the law of uneven and combined development; namely, that the proletariat might well come to power first in a backward country as a result of the contradictions of the world capitalist system as a whole. Both Lenin and Trotsky were firmly of the opinion that the victory of the revolution in such circumstances would prove to be only the prelude to the victory of the socialist revolution in the key capitalist countries and a means of facilitating the final outcome. It was in this spirit that the Bolsheviks took power in October 1917 and founded the Third International in 1919.

The revolution followed a more devious path than even its greatest theoreticians expected. We know what a heavy price mankind as a whole and the workers and peasants of the first workers' states in particular have had to pay for this detour.

The betrayals by the reformist bureaucracy led to the defeat of the German and Central European revolutions of 1918-21, isolating the first victorious revolution to backward Russia and thereby paving the way for the bureaucratic degeneration of the Soviet state and the Communist International, over which the Stalinist bureaucracy established tight control. The Comintern became transformed from an instrument of world revolution into an instrument of diplomatic maneuver in the hands of the Kremlin thereby blocking, first unintentionally, and then with calculated purpose, the victory of the proletarian revolution in many promising situations in many countries. At the end of World War II, Social Democratic and Stalinist class-collaborationist policies, in combination with the efforts of Western imperialism, led to the stabilization of a capitalist economy and a bourgeois state in several imperialist countries where the victory of socialism was objectively possible and even imminent.

As a result of the successive failure of the two major revolutionary waves of 1919-23 and 1943-48—and of the minor one of 1934-37—the main center of world revolution shifted for a time to the colonial world. The victory of the Chinese Revolution in 1949, following the

postwar revolutionary wave in Europe, opened an unin-
terrupted series of colonial revolutions. All the victorious
revolutions after 1917, including the establishment of workers' states through revolutionary upheavals in Yugoslavia,
China, Vietnam, and Cuba, thus took place in relatively
backward countries while the possibility of early revolutionary victory in the imperialist countries was postponed.

The view must be vigorously rejected that this development, unforeseen in the classics of Marxism, was more
or less fatally determined by objective factors or by lack
of revolutionary energy or will among the workers in the
imperialist countries. No one can seriously deny that since
1917 various mass upsurges and even uprisings of the
working class made the overthrow of capitalism objectively possible in many imperialist countries (Germany and
the whole of Central Europe 1918-20, Italy 1919-21,
Germany 1923, Britain 1926, Austria 1933-34, Spain
1931-37, Belgium 1932-36, France 1935-37, Italy 1943-
48, France 1944-48, Britain 1945-50, etc.). Nor can it
reasonably be denied that in innumerable general strikes,
occupations of factories, mass demonstrations that have
toppled governments, and even insurrections threatening
the foundations of bourgeois state power, that the proletariat of the imperialist countries (excepting the United
States) has shown again and again its understanding
of the general need to reconstruct society along socialist
lines and its willingness to carry out the task. The failure
of all these attempts is not due to any innate incapacity,
to any political "backwardness," or to "corruption," but
to the treacherous role of the offical leadership which
has repeatedly preferred not to utilize the objective possibility of taking power, or to deliberately destroy that
possibility. The European proletariat has been hit harder
by such betrayals than any other sector of the world
working class, as is clearly shown in the cases of Germany
and Spain.

The crisis of revolutionary leadership exists, of course,
in the colonial and semicolonial countries as well as in
the advanced countries. Many defeated or aborted revolutions bear witness to this crisis — from the Chinese Revolution of 1925-27 to the more recent defeats in Guatemala and Iraq. But in possible outcome of the struggle,

a big difference is evident between inadequate leadership in a backward country and similar leadership in an imperialist country: *the enemy facing the working population is immeasurably stronger in the latter.*

Confronted with the powerful and well-experienced bourgeoisie of the imperialist countries, the working class can achieve victory only under a genuine revolutionary Marxist leadership which is able: (1) to establish unity of action inside the ranks of the proletariat; (2) to mobilize to the fullest extent the latent and often hidden revolutionary potentialities of the working class; (3) to outmaneuver a very astute and supple capitalist class leadership which has learned how to transform reforms into a powerful brake upon revolutions; (4) to win over a part and neutralize another part of the petty bourgeoisie (the mass basis of capitalism in the imperialist countries) without surrendering its own class objectives. The absence of an explosive agrarian problem is an important element in strengthening and stabilizing capitalism in most imperialist countries.

The situation is different in the backward countries. Confronted by ruling classes, rotten to the core and lacking mass support, the revolution draws into struggle the mass of the working population, including the poorest peasants and pauperized petty bourgeoisie, bringing about collapse of the traditional order and its state, and exerting such pressure on centrist working-class parties and similar formations as to bring them to power.

Under anywhere near normal capitalist conditions, it should be remembered, "there do not," as Lenin said, "exist situations without a way out from an economic point of view." The failure of a revolutionary wave in an imperialist country gives way eventually to some form of temporary relative economic stabilization and even to fresh expansion. This inevitably postpones new revolutionary uprisings for a time, the combination of political setback (or even demoralization) of the working class and a rising standard of living being unfavorable for any immediate revolutionary undertaking.

In the colonial and semicolonial countries, on the other hand, the very weakness of capitalism, the whole peculiar socio-economic structure produced by imperialism, the permanent misery of the big majority of the population in the absence of a radical agrarian revolution, the stagnation and even reduction of living standards while industrialization nevertheless proceeds relatively rapidly, create situations in which the failure of one revolutionary wave does not lead automatically to relative or even temporary social or economic stabilization. A seemingly inexhaustible succession of mass struggles continues, such as Bolivia has experienced for ten years. The weakness of the enemy offers the revolution fuller means of recovery from temporary defeats than is the case in imperialist countries.

To sum up: the victories and defeats since 1917 express the relationship of forces between the old ruling class and the toiling masses on a world scale. The fact that the revolution won first in backward countries and not in the advanced is not proof that the workers in the advanced countries have shown insufficient revolutionary combativity. It is evidence of the fact that the opposition which they have to overcome in these countries is immeasurably stronger than in the colonial and semicolonial world. The weakness of the enemy in the backward countries has opened the possibility of coming to power even with a blunted instrument. The strength of the enemy in the imperialist countries demands a tool of much greater perfection.

At the same time, it is important to recognize that the three main forces of world revolution — the colonial revolution, the political revolution in the degenerated or deformed workers' states, and the proletarian revolution in the imperialist countries — form a dialectical unity. Each force influences the others and receives in return powerful impulses or brakes on its own development. The delay of the proletarian revolution in the imperialist countries has in general undoubtedly prevented the colonial revolution from taking the socialist road as quickly and as consciously as would have been possible under the influence of a powerful revolutionary upsurge or victory of the proletariat in an advanced country. This same delay also retards the maturing of the political revolution in the USSR, especially inasmuch as it does not place before the Soviet workers a convincing example of an alternative way to build socialism. Finally, the upsurge of the colonial and political revolutions, hampered by the delay of the proletarian revolution in the West, nevertheless contributes in helping the proletariat in the imperialist countries to overcome this delay.

2. The Colonial Revolution

From the close of World War II, and most noticeably after the victory of the Chinese Revolution, continual mass movements have drawn one backward country after another into the process of permanent revolution. The general causes of this wave are to be found in the weakening of the old colonial powers during and after World War II; the attraction exercised by the advances of the Soviet Union and especially the new China; the dawning mass awareness of the wretched material and moral conditions throughout these countries; the power displayed by the movement for national independence and its identification in the eyes of the masses with the possibility of overcoming misery, low living standards, low cultural levels, and exploitation and oppression of all kinds; the worsening of the international terms of trade for the countries exporting raw materials, especially since the end of the "Korean war boom"; the contrast between the enormous economic expansion of all the industrialized countries and the near stagnation (or lowering) of the standard of living of the masses in most of the colonial and semi-colonial countries in the past decade — these are some of the main causes of the general upheaval in the colonial world.

As a development in world history, the colonial revolution signifies above all that two billion human beings — men, women and children in areas where the tradition for centuries has been to live as passive subjects, condemned to super oppression and to super exploitation, utter humiliation and destruction of their national traditions and even their national identity, when they have not been made the target of mass slaughter and extermination — suddenly acquire a voice, a language and a personality of their own. Basically, the colonial revolution is the irrepressible tendency of these two billion human beings to become at last the masters and builders of their own destiny. The fact that this is socially possible only through a workers' state provides the objective basis for the tendency of the colonial revolution to move into the tracks of permanent revolution.

In the process of world revolution, the colonial revolution — first the Chinese Revolution and then the whole chain of upheavals — has prevented any temporary stabilization of the imperialist system on a world scale such as occurred after 1921. It has turned the international relationship of forces against capitalism, forced imperialism to fight — and in most cases lose — a series of defensive battles and wars, which it has launched in its efforts to halt the advance of world revolution in the colonial world. It has thereby given tremendous impetus to anticapitalist forces everywhere in the world. It has provided the Soviet Union and the other workers' states the necessary breathing spell needed to overcome the qualitative advance in the military field which came into the hands of imperialism as World War II reached its climax.

The colonial revolution could not by its own forces bring about the downfall of imperialism. Paradoxically, it has not even been able to undermine the relative economic stability of the imperialist countries. Contrary to the general revolutionary Marxist assumption following 1919, the collapse of the colonial system did not lead to an immediate economic crisis or breakdown in the imperialist countries; it coincided with the biggest relative expansion of capitalist production and foreign trade they have experienced in half a century.

Among the multiple causes of this apparent paradox, one is of outstanding importance. So long as the newly independent states, emerging through the colonial revolution, are held by bourgeois or petty-bourgeois leaderships within the limits of the capitalist mode of production and the capitalist world market, the real power of imperialism is not broken in these countries. *Its rule merely shifts from a direct to an indirect form.* As foreseen long ago by revolutionary Marxists, the basic strategy of imperialism, confronted with the colonial revolution, has been to modify its form of rule while seeking to maintain its essential content. In some cases, of course, this transformation has cost imperialism real losses and it has sought to avoid the dangerous shift in the form of its rule, sometimes by desperate and bloody colonial wars.

The transition from direct to indirect imperialist rule involves a redistribution of the surplus value produced by the colonial masses in favor of the colonial bourgeoisie and petty bourgeoisie at the expense of the imperialist power. Inasmuch as it also entails acceleration of the process of industrializing the colonial countries, it even signifies modification of the international division of labor, granting an increased share of the world market to the colonial bourgeoisie in the production of certain industrial consumer goods (especially textiles) and narrowing the imperialist countries in an increasing degree to the export of capital goods.

This aspect of neocolonialism corresponds to certain inherent needs of the imperialist bourgeoisie itself, the changing industrial structure forcing it to seek new markets for means of production rather than for consumption goods. So-called "aid to the underdeveloped countries" boils down to underwriting financially the effort to secure provisions for these needs, the expected political and social consequences being but by-products of successfully meeting the main economic necessity. But the limited nature of this industrialization process under bourgeois auspices, as well as the picayune amount of imperialist "aid," leave the real needs of economic development in the colonial countries scarcely touched. Basically their socio-economic structure thus remains as it was under direct imperialist rule. They continue substantially as producers and exporters of raw materials and food stuffs, completely dependent on the price fluctuations of the world market. They continue to carry the burden of tremendous unemployment or underemployment in the countryside. Even the limited industrialization process occurs at the cost of inflation and a lowering of real wages; i.e., at the cost of increased misery for the working masses.

Since the colonial revolution up to now has in the main been held within the framework of the capitalist world market, it has not inflicted staggering economic blows to the capitalist world economy as a whole, nor touched off major economic crises in imperialist countries which lost their former empires. Only one imperialist economy, because of its peculiar economic structure, seems doomed to collapse the moment it loses its colonial holdings — Portugal.

But this does not mean that the colonial revolution has not affected the mechanism of the imperialist economy. Its most noticeable consequence has been to slow down the export of private capital to the backward countries and to impel national or international public (government) bodies to assume the role normally undertaken by private capital in the heyday of imperialism. Grave monetary, financial, and economic contradictions flow from this. In the imperialist countries in the past ten years, the reluctance of private capital — in the face of relatively rapid expansion — to export its surpluses to backward countries caught up in the process of colonial revolution has constituted a major problem. Government investment guarantees and insurance can mitigate but not overcome the block.

As long as the great majority of the newly independent countries remain within the framework of the capitalist world market, these difficulties constitute a "lesser evil" from the viewpoint of world capitalism which can be handled, more or less, within the system — at least for the time being. *Only if the main semicolonial countries were to break out of the capitalist world system by becoming workers' states would the colonial revolution deliver economic blows of such proportions as to rapidly create the gravest economic and social crises in the imperialist centers.*

So far as real perspectives are concerned, it is not excluded that these countries will become workers' states before the political revolution triumphs in the Soviet Union and before the proletarian revolution scores a decisive victory in one or more of the important imperialist countries. However, it would be inadvisable for revolutionary socialists to base themselves on this unlikely variant. Such a perspective implies not only the continuation of the process of permanent revolution in the colonial world (which is sure to occur) but also *the victorious conclusion of this process in many countries within a specified time limit* (before victories elsewhere). A policy based arbitrarily upon any one of the many possible time sequences in the development of the three main sectors of the world revolution could lead to exceedingly grave political errors.

The objective conditions for the process of permanent revolution in the colonial countries rests basically on the inability of the colonial bourgeois or petty-bourgeois nationalist leaderships to solve, within the framework of the capitalist mode of production, fundamental problems created by economic and cultural upsurge. This is expressed most acutely by the incapacity of capitalism to undertake radical agrarian reform. The subjective conditions are determined by the fact that the colonial masses generally do not distinguish the conquest of national independence from the conquest of a high material and cultural standard of living. As long as living conditions do not improve, independence seems incomplete, inadequate, and even unreal. This means that *in the long run* no social, economic or political stabilization is possible in these countries without the victory of the socialist revolution. *Temporarily,* political stabilization can be achieved by bourgeois or petty-bourgeois nationalist leaderships which continue to be identified in the eyes of the masses with a real anti-imperialist struggle for national independence and which succeed in selling the masses the idea that the process of social upheaval and economic development is actually under way. The outstanding cases of relative success in this were Peron in Argentina, Nasser in Egypt, and Nehru in India. Even in these instances, the political equilibrium has proved to be quite unstable, indicating what would occur with the appearance of an alternative working-class leadership able to mobilize the general anti-imperialist feelings of the masses around basic, concrete, revolutionary goals which the traditional leadership cannot realize; for example, radical land reform in India.

For all these reasons, the most probable perspective for most of the backward countries is a succession of protracted social revolutionary crises which bourgeois or petty-bourgeois nationalist leaderships will desperately try to contain or to canalize, but which, despite inevitable setbacks, will periodically leap over these limits. This protracted period of instability and social crises does not imply the *automatic* victory of proletarian forces or of revolutionary peasant forces led by a Marxist leadership, that is, the *automatic* establishment of workers' states. As in the case of equating the *beginning* of the colonial revolution (under bourgeois or petty-bourgeois nationalist leadership) with its victorious *conclusion* under proletarian leadership, any idea that this process will occur automatically or inevitably within a certain time limit necessarily leads to a distorted estimate of the actual relationship of forces and replaces scientific analysis by illusions and wishful thinking. It presupposes that the objective process will by itself solve a task which can only be solved in struggle through the subjective effort of the vanguard: i.e., revolutionary-socialist conquest of the leadership of the mass movement. That this is possible in the very process of the revolution, and in a relatively short time, has been adequately demonstrated in the case of Cuba. That it is not inevitable, and that without it the revolution is certain to suffer serious defeats or be limited at best to inconclusive victories is demonstrated by much in the recent history of other Latin-American countries; for instance, Bolivia, Argentina and Guatemala.

A more precise perspective for each of the great ethneo-geographical zones of the colonial revolution (Latin America, the Arab world, Black Africa, the Indian subcontinent, and Southeast Asia) can only be worked out on the basis of a concrete analysis of the specific social and political forces at work and of their more exact economic conditions. However, certain general social trends, which apply to all or most of the colonial and semicolonial countries, can be indicated:

(a) The numerical and economic weakness of the national bourgeoisie. Despite the priority granted them by history, the national bourgeoisie has proved incapable of handling the capital made available under the rubric of "aid to the underdeveloped countries" in such a way as to achieve optimum results in industrialization. This is perhaps the biggest obstacle in the way of a "bourgeois solution" of the problem of economic underdevelopment. Everywhere we find the same phenomena: of available surplus capital, a major part is diverted from industrial uses to investment in land or usury, hoarding, import of luxury consumers goods, even outright flight abroad.

This incapacity of the national bourgeoisie is not the result, or mere reflection, of its moral corruption, but a normal operation of the capitalist drive for profits under the given economic and social conditions. Fear of permanent revolution is not the least of the motives involved.

(b) The creation of the infrastructure of heavy industry through the state, taking the form of nationalized property. The social layer heading and embodying this process is the urban petty bourgeoisie, especially the intellectuals, the military and state functionaries. The process favors, is even indispensable for, the development of a national bourgeois state. It can clash, however, with the interests of many parts of the old bourgeois classes in the private sector — not only the traditional compradore bourgeoisie but even the industrial bourgeoisie. This is the explanation for the anticapitalist demagogy and nationalizations of bourgeois enterprises undertaken in countries like Egypt, Ghana, etc. The functioning of the state in this field constitutes the objective basis for the "socialism" of Nehru and even Nasser, whatever the other differences between the two regimes. The general capitalist character of the economy remains clear cut in such countries, however, as long as (1) the state apparatus itself and the nationalized sectors remain feeding grounds for private accumulation of capital and private industrial enterprise (through corruption, theft, outright gifts, subsidies, etc.); (2) the national economy continues to be geared to the capitalist world market; (3) petty commodity production, constantly reproducing capital accumulation, prevails in the countryside.

(c) The strategic role of the colonial proletariat. In view of the peculiar socio-economic structure of these countries, the main strength of the proletariat does not lie among the industrial factory workers, who, with the exception of Argentina, form only a minority of the wage earners and a tiny fraction of the active working population of these countries. The colonial proletariat must be taken as the sum total of all those who live completely or essentially from the sale of their labor power; that is, industrial factory workers, public service workers, domestic workers, miners, plantation hands, agricultural workers, and the rural and urban workers who find only partial or occasional employment. The emphasis should

be placed on the latter four categories — the miners, plantation hands, agricultural workers and largely unemployed — typical for the colonial economy. They are numerically much stronger than generally supposed. Even in some countries of Black Africa (Rhodesia, South Africa, Angola, Congo) they constitute from one-fourth to three-fifths of the population. In the case of the Cuban Revolution, while poor peasants were the first recruits to the guerrilla forces, the base of the revolution shifted to field workers and rural unemployed, fusing finally with the proletariat of the sugar industry and the cities. Part of the explanation for the high level of consciousness that the Cuban Revolution rapidly attained lies in the composition of its mass base.

(d) The radical role of the peasantry. In the form of expanding guerrilla forces, the peasantry has undoubtedly played a much more radical and decisive role in the colonial revolution than was forecast in Marxist theory. It has revealed a social nature somewhat different from that of the traditional peasantry of the advanced capitalist countries. However, to prevent any misunderstanding or confusion, which in certain situations could lead to tragic errors (witness what happened in China after the introduction of the people's communes!), two basic distinctions must be made.

First, the distinction between the *revolutionary* role of the peasantry fighting for the conquest of land as private property (even though brought together through cooperatives) and the *conservative* role of the peasantry in the phase of the socialist transformation of property relations in the countryside. Experience in Eastern Europe and also in China has confirmed the lesson learned in Russia that wherever the peasantry stands in the forefront of the fight against the old landlord-usurer-compradore alliance in order to become master of the land, it can *as a class* be the ally of the proletariat only as long as the workers' state refrains from introducing socialist property relations in the countryside. Such relations can be based only on the *poorest* sector of the peasant class and can therefore be introduced only *gradually* in a country where agriculture prevails, if grave social crises are to be avoided. It should be noted, too, that the peasantry is not universally revolutionary. The existence of a large majority of small land-owning peasants has undoubtedly served as a momentary brake on the revolutionary process in several Southeast Asian countries (Malaya, Thailand, even Ceylon).

Second, the distinction between the *ingrained individualism* of the classical peasantry with a background of centuries of petty commodity production — either possessing land or aspiring to possess it; and the *predisposition* toward collectivism among rural populations still living under conditions of total or partial tribal (communal) property. This class, in contrast to the traditional peasantry, is not *per se* opposed to the introduction of socialist property relations in the countryside. It therefore remains an ally of the proletariat throughout the whole process of permanent revolution. In certain countries its existence can give a peasant uprising a powerful, semiproletarian character from the outset. Even in a favorable situation such as this, however, the level of consciousness of these masses should not be idealized. Miserably oppressed, having virtually literally "nothing to lose but their chains," these masses can offer humanity the most shining examples of revolutionary heroism and self-sacrifice. But only education under a capable Marxist leadership and a workers' state can make it possible for them to achieve revolutionary-socialist consciousness, especially the essential components of discipline, self-management and modern industrial rationality.

To win leadership among the colonial masses, the revolutionary Marxist vanguard must learn how to bring the basically progressive aspirations of the toiling masses into intimate connection with the program of revolutionary socialism. The constant struggle to educate the proletariat of the imperialist countries in the need to unconditionally support the colonial revolution must be linked with practical activity in bringing material aid to the colonial revolution. Among the freedom fighters in the colonial countries, it is a primary task to raise elementary revolutionary consciousness to the level of scientific socialism and an understanding of the dialectical interaction among the three main sectors of the world revolution today. All this cannot be achieved through some automatic process. It is an absolute necessity to educate revolutionary Marxist cadres and to build tendencies and independent parties wherever possible in all colonial countries. The building of sections of the Fourth International capable of working out concrete analyses of their specific national situations and finding concrete solutions to the problems remains a central strategic task in all countries.

To determine the place of the colonial revolution today in the general process of the world revolution, it is insufficient to take into consideration its consequences only in the politico-military field, where it has struck imperialism staggering blows, or in the economic area, where it has not yet seriously undermined the world economy of capitalism. We must also examine the effects of the colonial revolution on the relationship of class forces in the imperialist countries, particularly on the working-class movement, and on the conflicting social and political forces in the bureaucratically deformed or degenerated workers' states.

In most of the imperialist countries, the colonial revolution up to now has not significantly modified the relationship of forces to the expense of the bourgeoisie and the gain of the proletariat. However, in the case of France it was the Algerian Revolution which — by continuing in its heroic struggle against French imperialism despite the lack of help — prevented a decisive stabilization of the Bonapartist dictatorship of de Gaulle. The French working class, which received a terrible blow when de Gaulle came to power in May 1958, was given a breathing spell, precious time in which to recover its morale and begin to reassemble its forces. In Portugal, the outbreak of revolution in Angola and other colonies proved decisive in undermining the stability of the Salazar dictatorship, creating the prerevolutionary climate which has placed the overthrow of Portuguese fascism on the order of the day. The fall of Salazar would help accelerate the Spanish revolution, weaken the Bonapartist regime in France, and intensify the new wave of militancy in the West European labor movement.

Up to now the colonial revolution has not contributed directly toward radicalizing the mass movement in most imperialist countries; at best it has but increased the general consciousness, already widespread among significant layers, that the world capitalist system is growing relatively weaker. But it has affected elements in an immediate way, crystallizing new revolts against the waiting, passive, or treacherous attitude of the old leaderships toward the colonial revolution or fresh reactions against the generally low level of politics in some imperialist countries. This has occurred not only in France, where these new layers have been most vocal, but also in several other European countries, especially Spain, and in the United States where the opportunity to solidarize with the Cuban Revolution has opened the door to radical politics for a new generation of vanguard elements. In the same way the influence of the colonial revolution, especially the African revolution, upon vanguard elements in the Negro movement has helped prepare the emergence of a new radical left wing. In all these cases, it is the task of revolutionary Marxists to seek to win the best elements of this newly emerging vanguard to Trotskyism and to fuse them into the left wing of the mass movement.

The influence of the colonial revolution on the awakening masses of the workers' states has been complex and many-sided. In general the colonial revolution has helped to overcome lethargy and the feeling of political impotence. The interest displayed by these masses toward the colonial revolution (primarily the Chinese Revolution, but also the Algerian and Cuban revolutions since 1959) has been great and it is still increasing, along with feelings of solidarity. At the same time the problems raised by the antirevolutionary strategy of the Communist parties in both colonial and imperialist countries, and by the ambivalence which the ruling bureaucracies of the workers' states display toward the colonial revolution, have contributed toward political differentiation within the Communist parties of the workers' states, at first between sections of the youth and the bureaucracy, later between the Mao Tse-tung and Khrushchev factions. However, Mao Tse-tung's opportunistic and unprincipled bloc with the most conservative wing of the Soviet bureaucracy and his resistance to destroying the cult of Stalin, as particularly evidenced in the bloc with the Albanian CP leadership, has limited the extent and practical consequences of this differentiation among most CP's of the workers' states. An additional factor is the direct effect of the colonial revolution through such forces as colonial students who find it difficult to breathe in the monolithic atmosphere of the world Communist movement, and who at times pass beyond words to deeds to express their feelings as in the student demonstrations in Moscow and Sofia. The emergence of mass revolutionary forces led by parties or tendencies which have developed outside the realm of Stalinist control (Cuba, Algeria) has introduced a most powerful disintegrating element into international Stalinism, favoring the development of a revolutionary left wing.

If the direct economic and political effect of the colonial revolution has not been strongly felt in the imperialist countries, the establishment of workers' states in China, North Korea, Vietnam, and Cuba has had powerful ramifications among the Communist parties and in the formation of revolutionary leadership as a whole.

The Yugoslav and Chinese Communist parties failed to develop their "tendency" on a wide international scale for a number of specific reasons. The Yugoslavs sought a close, opportunistic alliance with the national bourgeoisie of the colonial and semicolonial countries. This effectively barred an alliance with the fighting elements of the colonial revolution. In Western Europe they took an opportunistic attitude toward the reformist bureaucracies, with parallel crippling effects on linking up with the revolutionary proletarian movement. Progressive developments inside Yugoslavia, however, have had considerable repercussions among the workers' states. For instance, "revival" of workers' councils has resounded especially in Poland and Hungary, even though this important step is limited by the fact that the councils do not wield political power.

The Chinese Communist Party has scored some successes among the Communist parties of the colonial world, where Peking has special appeal because of its antagonism to some (not all) of the national bourgeoisies. In the imperialist centers and in the workers' states, the Chinese appeal has been much more limited because of the unprincipled alliance with the unreconstructed Stalinists and because of the bureaucratic regime maintained in China. On these two key issues militant workers in the metropolitan centers, and workers, youth, and peasants of the workers' states, feel alienated from the Chinese. However, the criticisms levelled at Togliatti and similar figures have met with a favorable response among the ranks of many Communist parties.

The victory in Cuba marked the beginning of a new epoch in the history of the world revolution; for, aside from the Soviet Union, this is the first workers' state established outside the bounds of the Stalinist apparatus. Such a development, whatever the size of the country involved, was a turning point whose effects have necessarily reverberated on a tremendous scale throughout the whole world Communist movement.

In fact an international Castroist current has appeared inside the world Communist and revolutionary-socialist movement which, as was to be expected, is strongest in the colonial areas, especially Latin America and Africa. It is also noticeable in the other workers' states. In Algeria the influence of Castroism again testifies to the importance of the Cuban development.

Except in Spain and Portugal, Castroism has not had great impact in Europe. Its influence in other metropolitan centers such as the United States and Japan is likewise limited. One of the reasons for this is that the Cuban leadership has not yet reached an understanding of how it can best facilitate revolutionary rebirth in these areas.

The appearance of more workers' states through further development of the colonial revolution, particularly in countries like Algeria, would help strengthen and enrich the international current of Castroism, give it longer range perspectives and help bring it closer to understanding the necessity for a new revolutionary Marxist international of mass parties. Fulfillment of this historic possibility depends in part on the role which the Fourth International plays in the colonial revolution and the capacity of sections of the Fourth International to help win fresh victories.

The infusion of Trotskyist concepts in this new Castroist current will also influence the development of a conscious revolutionary leadership, particularly in the workers' states, will help prevent "Titoist" deviations and better assure the evolution of mass pressure and direct action into the cleansing force of political revolution. The development of the Portuguese and Spanish revolutions, historically possible in a short period, can also give rise to new tendencies of the Castroist type which would help the Cubans and related currents to achieve a fuller understanding of the process of world revolution in its entirety.

3. The Political Revolution

The mounting political passivity and apathy of the Soviet masses after 1923 was determined by two basic factors: the defeat of the international revolution and the consequent isolation of the first workers' state, and the low living standard of the masses due to the backwardness of Russia. These forced the Soviet masses to become preoccupied over the daily struggle to make ends meet. The feeling that under these same conditions the Soviet state remained in mortal danger of attack from world imperialism contributed to the political passivity.

Since the decisive turn in the world relationship of forces brought about by the victory of the Chinese Revolution, all the factors that favored political apathy among the Soviet masses have been steadily undermined; the conditions favoring a rise in mass political interest and militancy have been maturing. The isolation of the first workers' state has been broken, not only in Europe, but in Asia and the whole world. The rapid rise in the living standards of the masses since Stalin's death — a result of growing mass pressure on the bureaucracy under conditions of increased technological and economic progress — has enabled the people to devote part of their energies to cultural and political aims. The emergence of the Soviet Union as the second industrial power of the world, even holding the lead in several technological fields, has made its relatively low standard of living all the more incongruous and has served to stimulate increased economic demands. The threat of imperialist attack remains, and the bureaucracy uses this threat quite consciously to periodically silence the voices of opposition. However, the masses cannot help but feel the new power and standing of the Soviet Union in world affairs in the epoch of missile warfare, when the leaders of the bureaucracy themselves continually boast of their ability to inflict a crushing defeat on the imperialist warmongers.

The evolution of the workers' states as a whole since the victory of the Chinese Revolution in 1949, and especially after Stalin's death in 1953, has therefore steadily removed the causes that fostered political passivity among the masses and their vanguard. In the East European workers' states this development was hastened, although made more complex, by a strong feeling of national oppression among the masses. All these new factors contributed to such events as the June 16-17, 1953, general strike and uprising in Eastern Germany, to the Poznan events in the spring of 1956 in Poland, to the beginning of the political revolution in Poland and Hungary in October 1956, to the renewal of political militancy among some layers of the workers' vanguard and oppositional Communists during the "hundred flowers bloom" period in China in early 1957, to the increasing pressure of the Soviet masses on the bureaucracy which won the concessions of 1953 (breaking up of the GPU power, dissolution of the slave-labor camps and a radical modification of the oppressive factory labor code), then the denunciation of the Stalin cult in 1956 at the Twentieth Congress of the Soviet CP and a continuous rise since 1953 in the mass standard of living as a result of radical changes in the bureaucracy's general economic policy, and finally the important new political concessions granted at the Twenty-second Congress (new political rights written into the new party program, partial public rehabilitation of the victims of Stalin's purges, etc.).

Mass pressure in the Soviet Union began with a general revolt against the most barbaric and arbitrary forms of Stalin's Bonapartist dictatorship, in which all social layers participated. The pressure then began to become differentiated in the economic field, all social layers participating, but each with its own set of demands. From this, the movement advanced toward specific political demands, first from the ranks of the bureaucracy who demanded and obtained a stabilizing of conditions for the bureaucrats as individuals. This was done by widening the participation in the exercise of political power. These reforms were welcomed by the workers. The first rumblings from the peasantry were demands for kolkhoz [collective farm] democracy, voiced publicly here and there in the Soviet Union. The ferment among the intellectuals and students, which is expressed around such issues as freedom in art and scientific research, foreshadows demands for political democracy. Certain sectors of the bureaucracy have indicated awareness of the objective need to loosen the Stalinist stranglehold on the productive forces, the better to meet the threatening military and technological advances of U. S. imperialism.

As yet, such key demands as workers' management in the factories and the establishment of control through democratically elected councils have not been raised. But it is only a question of time until they begin to appear. One reason for the sensitivity of the Soviet bureaucracy toward "Yugoslav revisionism" is fear of the attraction which Yugoslav experimentation with workers' councils and self-management can hold for the advanced Soviet workers, youth, intellectuals, and even the lower layers of the bureaucracy, especially the lower ranks of the trade-union officialdom, who are in direct contact with the proletariat.

It is necessary to distinguish clearly between generalized mass pressure, the beginning of mass actions (invariably of reformist character), and the opening of the real political revolution. This distinction is not always easily made in the heat of events since it involves successive stages of one and the same process, each linked to the next and without clear boundary lines. This was clearly borne out in the case of the Polish events in 1956 and the actions leading to the first phase of the Hungarian Revolution. Nevertheless, a few generalizations can be made concerning the Soviet Union.

In the first place, the dominant trend since 1953 has been *mass pressure* rather than *mass action*. There are some outstanding exceptions: the revolt at Vorkuta and other slave-labor camps probably played a decisive role in hastening the liquidation of this whole utterly reactionary system. Some local strikes wrenched considerable concessions for the workers in housing and better distribution of consumer goods. Certain actions by students, youth groups, and vanguard intellectuals may have contributed in bringing about the political concessions made to the masses at the Twenty-second Congress. But in general the pressure on the bureaucracy has remained below the level of mass actions. The pressure of a formidable mass of people, slowly awakening to political life, is of course a sufficient nightmare to the bureaucracy to wring substantial concessions.

Far from satisfying the masses and lulling them into apathy, the concessions have only whetted appetites. The discontent of the masses over their low standard of living is certainly more vocal, if not actually greater in force, than it was before Stalin's death. Such a seemingly paradoxical phenomenon is well known in capitalist countries. What the concessions have gained for the bureaucracy is a *general reformist atmosphere*, especially since the Hungarian events, an atmosphere in which the masses expect that continued pressure will be rewarded by substantial new concessions. They do not yet see the need or possibility of broader mass actions, the scope of which would reach revolutionary proportions.

This atmosphere can perhaps last for some time, but it will not last forever. Two forces inherent in the current dialectical relations between mass pressure and bureaucratic reforms tend to undermine it. The first force is the inclination of the masses to convert into reality the political rights conceded to them on paper. At a certain point this can lead to open collision with powerful sectors of the bureaucracy. The second force is the tendency of mass demands to evolve into demands for workers' control and workers' management. Pressure along this line was reflected in a manifest way for the first time in the Central Committee of the Communist Party at its November 1962 plenum. In fact, the greater the concessions before the stage of open clashes is reached, and the stronger the Soviet economy becomes, the more decisive will be the character of the clashes and the more favorable the relationship of forces for the masses at the time of the political revolution.

In analyzing the interaction between the three components of the world revolution — the colonial revolution, the political revolution (above all in the Soviet Union), and the proletarian revolution in the imperialist countries — the *time element* is of decisive importance. Even without the restoration of proletarian democracy, the Soviet Union exercises enormous attractive power on the masses of the colonial countries — if only because the Soviet Union proves what can be done in less than a half century to bring a backward country up to the level of an advanced industrial country in economic development and improved standard of living. Should a revolutionary-socialist leadership resume power in the Soviet Union in the not too distant future, with the consequent establishment of socialist democracy internally and revolutionary solidarity abroad, the process of *fusing the colonial revolution with the workers' states would be tremendously speeded up*.

This would take a double form in practice. The new Soviet leadership would end Moscow's general current strategy which is to depend on *alliances with the colonial bourgeoisie*. Naturally the new leadership would continue the Leninist policy of giving critical support and material assistance to bourgeois or petty-bourgeois nationalist leaderships in open conflict with imperialism. What it would put a stop to is the reactionary policy of subordinating the revolutionary vanguard to the national bourgeoisie. Removing this source of political and material strength would hasten loss of control by the colonial capitalist class over the decisive sectors of mass opinion. The other side of the same policy would be rejection of the opportunist leadership in control of most of the Communist parties in the colonies today, whose main strength lies in identification with the Soviet Union. The new Soviet leadership would assist those oppositional forces within the Communist parties that want to make a decisive turn to the left, or it would support the new revolutionary proletarian forces now springing up outside the traditional Communist parties, especially in countries where they are either very weak or utterly compromised in the eyes of the colonial masses because of their past errors or betrayals. In both ways the conquest of leadership of the colonial revolution by genuine revolutionary proletarian forces would be greatly facilitated and along with it, under favorable objective conditions, the tendency of the colonial revolution to end in the establishment of workers' states would be greatly accelerated.

An early victory of the political revolution in the Soviet Union would at the same time hasten the process of proletarian revolution inside the imperialist countries in an even more decisive manner. The reestablishment of Soviet democracy in the USSR on a higher level — signifying for the first time since the early twenties a regime of real democracy and intellectual freedom, qualitatively superior to the most democratic bourgeois states — would end at one stoke the main objection against communism held by class-conscious workers of the imperialist countries. It would lead rapidly to the disappearance of the bureaucratic Stalinist leadership in the old CP's, which would split in various directions, principally into a left-reformist wing and a genuine revolutionary-socialist wing. In countries like France and Italy, where the Communist parties, despite their opportunism, continue to control the mass movement, this would mean rapid development of a revolutionary mass party which would put the proletarian conquest of power on the agenda at the first favorable objective occasion. In countries where the Communist parties are weak secondary forces, it would favor the emergence of a revolutionary-socialist mass movement through the fusion of the left wing in the Social Democratic parties — attracted by the reborn Soviet democracy — and the best elements among the old CP militants. In this way the crisis of revolutionary leadership could eventually be overcome and new objectively revolutionary situations would open the road for the victory of the proletariat.

However entrancing the picture of the worldwide consequences of an *early* victory of the political revolution in the Soviet Union may be, the process may prove to be longer drawn out than we desire. It would of course be an error for Marxist revolutionary forces to stake everything on this one card, meantime overlooking the very real opportunities for breakthroughs in the colonial and imperialist countries before the political revolution in the USSR succeeds. Consequently, it is advisable to take into account the effect which continuous technological and economic progress of the USSR and the other workers' states can have on the world revolutionary process in the absence of an early victory.

As already stated, the continuous economic and cultural rise of the workers' states has an important effect in undermining the confidence of the colonial masses in any "capitalist way" of solving the problem of underdevelopment and in increasing their confidence in the socialist solution of this problem. Economic progress, especially of the Soviet Union, increases the weight of the workers' states in the world economy, enabling them to break the imperialist monopoly of buying primary products from many backward countries, and putting them in position to offer an attractive alternative to the onerous imperialist grants of equipment and development projects. The further technological and economic advance of the workers' states objectively favors the colonial revolution and the tendency, in the throes of this revolution, to break away from the capitalist world market. The example of Cuba shows this very clearly. It is evident that the sudden imperialist blockade and attempt to force Cuba to its knees when Washington refused to buy any more Cuban sugar would have been enormously more effective if the USSR and China had not been able to come forward as alternative customers.

The increasing weight of the workers' states on the world market is quite far as yet from enabling them to play a larger role than imperialism in the foreign trade of the backward countries as a whole. It is little likely that the combined economic power of the workers' states will surpass the combined economic power of the highly industrialized countries of the West for some years to come, unless of course a revolutionary victory occurs in the main imperialist sector. It must not be forgotten that the USSR and China are not economically complementary to the underdeveloped countries to such a high degree as are the West European capitalist powers. It should also be observed that as long as the political revolution does not score a decisive victory in the USSR, the Soviet bureaucracy will not be prone to utilize to the fullest extent the revolutionary possibilities that are opened up with the increasing economic power of the workers' states, since this conflicts with the orientation of an alliance with the colonial bourgeoisie.

The view that the economic and technological advances of the workers' states can in themselves decisively modify the relationship of forces between the classes in the imperialist countries, or contribute decisively to the overthrow of capitalism in these countries, must be rejected as false. The positive results of such advances upon capitalist society in the West can be felt objectively in increased competition for foreign markets for some industrial products, and subjectively in the slow disappearance of many reactionary prejudices against communism which were created or aroused by the crimes of Stalinism. The subsidence of prejudices will become more noticeable as the living standards of the Soviet masses come closer to those of Western Europe. But neither effect is sufficient to rehabilitate small and discredited Communist parties or to miraculously swing the opportunistic bureaucratic leadership of the mass Communist parties in France, Italy, and Greece into a revolutionary orientation.

The main contribution to the development of the proletarian revolution in the imperialist countries remains therefore the effect in the labor movement of the crisis of Stalinism and the technological and economic gains of the USSR. This is evident in the growing differentiation inside the Communist parties, the possibility of real mass opposition tendencies developing within some of these parties, the increased possibility of mergers between the revolutionary Marxist vanguard and the leftward-moving mass of militants in some of these parties, and the rapid disappearance of anti-Trotskyist prejudices inside many Communist parties as a result of the decisions of the Twentieth and Twenty-second Congresses.

4. The Proletarian Revolution in the Imperialist Countries

Since the postwar revolutionary upsurge in Western Europe and the postwar strike wave in the United States, great changes have taken place in the labor movement and in the objective conditions it faces in the imperialist countries. Contrary to the expectations of both Marxist and non-Marxist economists, the capitalist economy of the advanced industrialized countries, including Japan, underwent an expansion not experienced since World War I, i.e., for nearly half a century. The interaction of such economic growth and the treacherous opportunist policies of the traditional working-class leaderships in Western Europe and the trade union bureaucracy in the U.S., in the absence of an alternative revolutionary leadership, made possible the temporary relative stabilization of capitalism in Europe. The main center of the revolutionary movement thereupon shifted for the time being to the colonial countries.

This temporary development fostered both revisionist and defeatist views of the proletarian revolution in the imperialist countries. Each of these standpoints rules out the possibility of the proletariat realistically struggling for power in the West for a long time to come. Since it is impossible not to note that the general world trend is running against capitalism, protagonists of these concepts expect essentially *outside forces* to eventually overcome capitalism in the imperialist centers. A theory current in leading circles among many Communist parties is that the economic progress of the USSR will eventually solve the problem of winning socialism in the West. When the living standard of the Soviet people rises above the living standards of the West European and North American workers, then these workers will automatically turn toward communism. Another theory, voiced more or less consciously by ideologists like Sweezy and Sartre, is that the colonial revolution will eventually bring down imperialism and that the vanguard in the advanced capitalist countries cannot play a much bigger role than actively aiding the colonial revolutionists.

Both theories are based on a single wrong assumption; i.e., that it is impossible for the Western proletariat to fulfill its historic mission in the next decades. This pessimistic assumption is then made less bitter by assuming that there are other alternatives which should be taken as goals of action. Under careful analysis, however, the imagined alternatives do not stand up as realistic.

Even if the USSR's per capita production overtakes that of the United States within the next ten years, at least another decade will be needed to overtake the U.S. per capita standard of living, since this is a combination of current production and past accumulation of consumer goods and public welfare provisions. A catastrophic fall in the living standard of the American and West European workers due to a major economic crisis would, of course, change this perspective. But then it is obvious that the revolutionary consequences of the crisis would be much more important than the attractive power that might be exercised by Soviet economic growth.

Even if the USSR's per capita standard of living becomes the highest in the world, it does not follow that this in itself would break down capitalism in the West, for it would not automatically lead to depressions, economic decline, and a lowering of the workers' standard of living. Those who defend this theory start from the wrong assumption that the proletariat in the West is basically "satisfied" with the present economic "prosperity" and lacks awareness of the deeper aspects of the alienation that permeates capitalist society.

As for the capacity of the colonial revolution by itself to cause the downfall of Western imperialism — we have already analyzed the reasons why this is an unrealistic perspective.

The truth is that both these defeatist theories concerning the revolutionary potential of the Western proletariat lead in the final analysis to the absurd conclusion that imperialism is still assured of a long period of stable existence.

The basic fallacy in all variations of these theories is their crude mechanistic economic determinism. The unspoken premise is that a working class enjoying a relatively high standard of living is unwilling or unable to fight for the overthrow of capitalism. The assumption is groundless both theoretically and empirically. On the level of theory it should be clear that the attitude of the workers is determined by many forces, among which the *absolute level* of the standard of living is only one among other determinants. It makes a world of difference whether a high standard of living is the result of working-class struggles, and therefore appears as *a series of conquests that must be defended* or whether it appears to the workers to be a "gift" from a "beneficent" set of masters. In the first case a high standard of living can give powerful impulsion to militancy rather than acting as a brake; in the second case a high standard of living can have a demoralizing effect, feeding the class-collaborationist illusions cultivated by the bourgeois spokesmen and the ideologists of the right wing of the labor movement. On the empirical level, Marx gathered considerable material showing the revolutionary effect on the British workers when they won the ten-hour day in the past century. Rosa Luxemburg called attention to the revolutionary effect of all fundamental trade-union achievements. Recent strike waves in Belgium, Spain, and Italy — spearheaded by the *best-paid workers* — again proves that it is quite false to hold that the highest paid workers are automatically "corrupted" by "capitalist prosperity."

What both theory and experience do prove is that the most revolutionary consequences follow not so much from the *absolute level* of real wages and living standards as from their *relative short-term fluctuations*. Attempts to lower even slightly a hard-won high level, or the widespread fear that such an attempt is in preparation, can under certain conditions touch off great class actions that tend to pass rapidly from the defensive to the offensive stage and put on the agenda struggles of an objectively prerevolutionary significance around transitional slogans. Such struggles may even lead to revolutionary situations.

Two generations of revolutionists in the West have been educated in the belief that revolutionary situations in industrialized countries coincide with big crises or complete breakdowns of the capitalist economy and state such as occur in war or military defeat (Germany and Central Europe after World War I, Greece, France, and Italy after World War II). But again theory and history prove that this is but one road to possible revolutionary crisis in a highly developed industrial country. The big strike wave of 1936-37, and along with it the Spanish Revolution, came neither at the end of a war nor at the peak of a major economic breakdown. They came in the period of relative economic recovery between the two big crises of 1929 and 1938. A whole series of contributing factors — the most important being the threat of fascism and the desire of the workers to make up for the suffering borne during the big economic crisis — gave this strike wave a prerevolutionary character in the U.S. and Belgium and a revolutionary challenge in France. In the imperialist countries in the next five to ten years such revolutionary crises and opportunities are much more likely to occur than crises of the breakdown type of 1918-19 or 1944-48.

No Marxist, of course, will deny that a long period of economic "prosperity" brings changes in the proletariat's mode of life and thought. Habits formed during long periods of misery — indifference toward personal property in consumer goods, the tendency to express immediate solidarity in sharing money, the acceptance of daily sacrifices as normal, the indifference and hostility toward many institutions and the whole superstructure of capitalism — gradually disappear. New habits and ways of thinking appear which, to superficial observers, seem "petty bourgeois." It is a mistake, however, to approach these changes from an abstract "moral" point of view — the idealization of misery, degradation, and the reduction of needs to purely physiological levels is wrong in theory and very dangerous in practice! New ways of thinking and acting are important *only as they serve to retard or advance the class struggle under given conditions*. The automobile of the American workers — taken not so long ago by many people as the symbol of the "petty-bourgeois mentality of the American proletariat" — became the instrument of a completely new and radical strike technique at the end of World War II. The scooter and motorbike of the European workers appeared during the Belgian general strike in the form of flying strike squads, an embryo of the future revolutionary defense guards of the Belgian proletariat.

If some of the obviously fine qualities of the under-nourished proletariat of yesterday seem to have disappeared among Western workers, other good new qualities have appeared, precisely as a result of the higher standard of living and culture gained by the proletariat in the West. The gap between the knowledge of the skilled worker and bourgeois technician has virtually disappeared or been greatly reduced. Technologically, Western workers are much more capable of socialist self-management today than were their parents or grandparents, and they feel more strongly the need to play a conscious leading role in the process of production.

It is also easier for today's worker to reach an understanding of the over-all economic interaction among all the factors, the intertwining of all economic problems, and the needs and practical purposes of socialist planning. The increase in leisure time in many countries also means the increased possibility to participate on a mass scale in political administration, something that never existed in the past. It is not for Marxists to deny the basic Marxist truth that capitalism is the great educator of the workers for socialism, at least on the economic field.

The mechanism through which prerevolutionary or even revolutionary situations can arise in the framework of the relatively stabilized capitalist economies of the Western imperialist countries can be briefly stated as follows:

After a first period of rapid economic expansion fed essentially by the war preparations, by the need for reconstruction (both absolute and relative; i.e., rebuilding destroyed cities and plants, modernizing outmoded equipment) in Europe and Japan, and by the big wave of technological revolution spurred by both reconstruction and preparations for a new world war, the economies of the imperialist countries have now entered a period in which the forces of expansion are slowly spending themselves, and in which competition among the newly equipped imperialist countries is sharpening in a world market that is relatively smaller as a result of the victories in the colonial revolution and the economic expansion of the workers' states. This increased competition, heightened still further by the constitution of the Common Market in Western Europe, will strengthen the inevitable tendency for the average rate of profit to decline. (In the final analysis this tendency is a consequence of the new technological revolutions; i.e., of the higher organic composition of capital.)

In reaction to these tendencies, the capitalist class will seek periodically to ameliorate its positions in the competitive struggle by slowing down the rate of increase of real wages, by freezing wages, or even by trying to reduce real wages, especially in the imperialist countries where the workers enjoy the highest relative wages. The response of the proletariat to these attacks can lead to great struggles that will tend to move toward prerevolutionary and even revolutionary situations, provided that the working class, or at least its broad vanguard, has sufficient self-confidence to advance the socialist alternative to the capitalist way of running the economy and the country. This in turn hinges essentially on the activity and influence of a broad left wing in the labor movement that educates the vanguard in the necessity of struggling for this socialist alternative and that builds up self-confidence and an apparatus capable of revolutionary struggle through a series of successful partial struggles.

This is, of course, only a generalized pattern in which various particular variants should be included: the possibility of the working class reacting violently against an attempt to limit or suppress its fundamental political and trade-union rights (against an attempt to impose a "strong" state or against an emergent fascist danger); the possibility of a swift reaction to a sudden financial or political crisis; the possibility of mass opposition against an attempt to launch a new colonial war, or against general preparations for war, etc. The essential point for revolutionary Marxists is to link up the program of revolutionary socialism with the masses through a series of transitional demands corresponding to the specific conditions of each country and through intimate ties with the mass movement. The objective is to stimulate and broaden mass struggles to the utmost and to move as much as possible toward playing a leading role in such struggles, beginning with the most elementary demands and seeking to develop them in the direction of transitional slogans on the level of government power and the creation of bodies of dual power. (Labor to Power; For a Workers' Government; A Workers' and Peasants' Government; A Workers' Government Based on the Trade Unions; and other variants.)

In the United States the wave of working-class militancy which can lead to a decisive turn in the domestic situation will in all likelihood follow a comparable pattern. It will come about as the capitalist class undermines its alliance with the trade-union bureaucracy by starting to pass on to the American working class the cost of measures required to counteract the chronic deficit of the balance of payments, mounting inflation, and depreciation of the dollar accompanied by suppression of escalator clauses in collective contracts, attempts to freeze or lower real wages in order to improve the competitive position in foreign markets, increases indirect taxation of low and medium incomes, etc. The long-range tendency toward rising permanent unemployment and the relative whittling down of trade union strength will add to the ferment. The first major moves of the capitalist class against the working class could touch off a tremendous defensive reaction, forcing some union leaders to break their alliance with the Democratic Party and finally opening up the road for the appearance of a mass labor party.

The most probable variant in the next few years is, therefore, the following: the colonial revolution will continue, involving new countries and deepening its social character as more workers' states appear. It will not lead directly to the overthrow of capitalism in the imperialist centers, but it will play a powerful role in building a new world revolutionary leadership as is already clear from the emergence of Castroist currents. The pressure of the masses in the workers' states will continue, with a tendency toward increasing mass action and the possible beginning of political revolution in several workers' states. Both these developments will favorably influence the resurgence of mass militancy among the proletariat in the imperialist countries, reinforcing a tendency stemming directly from the socio-economic mechanism of advanced capitalism and the slowing down of its rate of expansion.

The possibility of a working-class victory in an imperialist country—not just Portugal or Spain, but the other West European countries and Japan, Australia, and Canada—thus exists in the next decade. A victory in any of these countries would in turn hasten the victory of the political revolution in the key country, the USSR, if it had not already occurred, and these would react in turn to speed the victory of the American revolution. The victory of the socialist revolution in any of the advanced countries would play a decisive role in developing the economies of the backward countries at the most rapid possible rate.

Since the close of World War II, the imperialist powers have been engaged in feverish preparations for a third conflict. In fact imperialism has engaged in virtually constant wars, on a larger or smaller scale, in its effort to stem the advance of world revolution: the wars in China, Vietnam, Indonesia, Malaya, Kenya, Korea, Suez, Algeria, Laos, Angola, plus such interventions as Eisenhower's moves in Guatemala and Lebanon and Kennedy's invasion of Cuba at Playa Giron. The master plan of launching nuclear war on the USSR and China reached dangerous levels on several occasions during the past fifteen years: during the opening stages of the cold war, again during the American invasion of North Korea, at the battle of Dien Bien Phu, during the Suez crisis, the 1960 Berlin crisis, and finally and most ominously during the fall 1962 crisis over Cuba.

Several conjunctural factors explain why imperialism has not yet launched a full-scale atomic world war. Economic expansion was still possible with the help of periodic waves of rearmament; no major economic crisis loomed as an immediate threat; the hope still exists of diverting the colonial revolution through a de facto alliance with an apparently "neutralist" colonial bourgeoisie. (An example is the so-called "neutral" solution of the Laos question, in which the Soviet bureaucracy assists American imperialism to impose a halt on the Laos revolution.)

Other considerations gave the American imperialists pause, forcing them to postpone their timetable. At the end of World War II, the American armed forces proved unreliable for any further wars. In the face of great protest strikes and "Get Us Home" demonstrations, they had to be brought back to the United States and a totally new force constructed. In addition, possible domestic political opposition to another war had to be contained and reduced. The years of McCarthyism cut deeply into democratic rights and civil liberties in the U. S. but it is still doubtful that the public is really conditioned to accept another world war. The experience in Korea was very revealing in this respect. It rapidly became the most unpopular war in American history, and the adventure had to be brought to a halt. The colonial revolution has played a similar role by helping to bring the Negro movement in the United States increasingly into the political arena as a potentially strong independent force which could easily link up with any moves toward a labor party among the trade unions and political opposition to another world war. The possibility of American troops becoming "contaminated" by revolutionary ideas through contact with the forces against which they must be pitted also enters into the calculations which have caused American imperialism to hesistate at going over the brink into another world war.

In addition, nuclear war brings a new element to bear in war as an extension of politics—the very real possibility of suicide. A war that promises self-destruction loses its main purpose—which is victory and enjoyment of the spoils of conquest. The American imperialists have brandished the H-bomb for many years but still find themselves not quite capable of emulating Hitler in setting the torch to the funeral pyre they have put together. Thus, much as certain warmongers urge the rulers holding decisive power to take the final plunge, they have felt a still stronger compulsion to postpone the final reckoning.

Conscious of the danger that the capitalist system now faces of going down altogether, its statesmen have sought to strengthen it internally since the end of World War II. Behind the major policies of world capitalism is the view that survival of the system can be assured, or its demise postponed, only through a worldwide strategy of defense against the forces of the world proletarian revolution. The main capitalist countries and the satellites tied to them through interlocking military alliances (NATO, SEATO, etc.) have been acting as a world capitalist police force.

But while American imperialism must necessarily mobilize world capitalism as a whole for the assault on the workers' states, and must especially mobilize Western Europe and Japan, the capitalist system is far from monolithic. The old imperialist powers like Britain and France, reduced to the status of mere satellites to the American colossus, may well find it highly profitable to prepare for war and to accept the American handouts needed to shore up their structures. Experience has taught them, however, that war itself is not necessarily as profitable as its preparation. And this elementary truth holds especially in the case of nuclear war, which can end in the destruction of all the higher forms of life on this planet, including the capitalists. They thus exhibit a strong tendency to drag their feet as doomsday draws nearer. A sudden move by a de Gaulle exposes unexpectedly deep fissures in the capitalist alliances and new doubts are thrust upon the rulers of the West.

Insofar as changes in the relationship of forces due to the colonial revolution, the class struggle in the capitalist countries, the economic situation of capitalism, or the economic progress of the workers' states do not threaten to put an immediate end to capitalism, a new compromise is always possible between the heads of the two main opposing camps. As long as they do not face an immediate major threat, both U.S. imperialism and the Soviet bureaucracy will remain facing each other, striving to gain better positions or to avoid falling into worse ones, to strengthen their economic and military power, to acquire new allies or to avoid losing old ones, always seeking a compromise when the opponent appears ready to plunge into war. It is a dangerous game. How secure is the "security space" that each side tries to keep in reserve? It can be punctured at any time by an "error" or by a "misunderstanding" or by an act of mad folly.

In the face of nearly unanimous scientific opinion that a full-scale nuclear world war would signify the complete destruction of human civilization, if not the very physical existence of all mankind, it is obvious that the central strategic goal of the world labor movement cannot be a speculative victory in an atomic world war. To build communism, mankind must exist. A certain minimum material infrastructure is also necessary. Any assumption that "communist consciousness" is sufficient to build communism in a world of radio-active ruins, drops below the level of the primitive pre-Marxist utopians. *The goal must be to prevent an atomic world war.*

For a time, the development of Soviet nuclear weapons was a necessary step toward prevention of a nuclear world war. Without the Soviet A-bomb, a world war would have certainly broken out as a consequence of the local wars in either Korea or Vietnam. But at a certain point, the only means of preventing a nuclear world war is *the disarmament of imperialism by the workers of the imperialist countries.* This is feasible since atomic weapons cannot be used in a civil conflict without the capitalist class committing mass suicide — an outcome of remote possibility despite the appearance of such insane slogans as "Better dead than red."

A world nuclear war is not inevitable. The realistic alternative is to disarm imperialism by overthrowing it in its main bastions. The interacting process of colonial revolution, political revolution in the workers' states, and proletarian revolution in the imperialist countries has this as one of its end results. The development of this process operates in a dual way on the outlook of the imperialists. As the revolutionary forces grow stronger, the imperialists become less and less confident in their own ultimate perspective and more hesitant about staking everything on nuclear war. On the other hand the very same development increases their tendency to close their eyes to the future. When they feel that no other alternative is open but passive capitulation before the revolution, they are capable of plunging into a fatal adventure. But at a certain point the momentum of the class struggle will place the workers in the imperialist countries in position to intervene in time and prevent imperialism from unleashing nuclear war.

In the final analysis only the victory of the proletariat in the most highly developed imperialist countries, above all the victory of the American proletariat, can free mankind definitively from the nightmare of nuclear annihilation. This is the revolutionary-socialist solution that the Fourth International counterposes to the utopian illusions of "peaceful coexistence" and "victory" in a nuclear world war. The classical alternative, socialism or barbarism, today boils down to a socialist America or the nuclear destruction of the human race.

In this way revolutionary Marxism today brings to all sectors of the world proletariat a single integrated concept of world revolution, full support to wars of liberation waged by colonial peoples being an important contribution to the coming disarmament of imperialism by the proletariat of the imperialist countries. For the same reason, transitional slogans of a unilateral pacifist nature in the imperialist countries, far from being "reactionary" or "utopian," as old-time pacifism was, can play an extremely progressive role provided that they are linked with other transitional slogans culminating in the working-class struggle for power.

5. The Fourth International

The year 1963 marks the twenty-fifth anniversary of the Fourth International and nearly four decades since the label of "Trotskyism" began to be attached to revolutionary socialism. In ideas, our movement has been very productive, more than justifying its existence by this alone. In its programmatic declarations and in its participation in the class struggle on a worldwide scale it has proved itself to be the legitimate heir and continuator of the great tradition of revolutionary Marxism. Events have proved it right on so many points that even its antagonists have had to borrow from its arsenal, though in a partial, one-sided, or distorted way.

The struggle led by Leon Trotsky and the Left Opposition for rapid planned industrialization of the USSR as the only means to prevent the kulak from undermining the socialist mode of production in industry and the monopoly of foreign trade was vindicated as early as 1927-28. Hardly anyone in the world labor movement today doubts the correctness of the Trotskyist struggle against Stalin's notorious theory and practice of "social fascism" in the early thirties, which paved the way for Hitler. The Trotskyist critique of the theory and practice of "popular frontism" has been shown to be correct in the most painful way, again and again, by the unnecessary defeats suffered by the working class when objective conditions were most favorable for victory, as in France and Spain in 1935-37; in France, Italy, and Greece in 1943-48; etc.

The Trotskyist exposures and denunciations of the crimes of Stalin in the thirties have now finally had their belated echo in official Soviet doctrine, beginning with Khrushchev's admissions at the Twentieth Congress of the CPSU. The validity of the Trotskyist explanation of the character of the bureaucracy as a *social force* has become accepted by all serious students of the Soviet Union. It is even reflected in the theoretical basis and justification offered by the Yugoslav government in its experimentation with workers' councils and self-management. The correctness of the Trotskyist struggle for the revival of the Leninist norms of proletarian democracy in the Soviet Union received striking confirmation in the more or less spontaneous appearance of workers' councils at the very beginning of the political revolution in Poland and Hungary in October 1956.

The timeliness of even some of the oldest Trotskyist positions is graphically shown by the following case: In 1923 Trotsky held that if a certain degree of bureaucratization of a workers' state in an underdeveloped country is objectively inevitable, then it is the task of a revolutionary party to *limit* this to the utmost by developing all the objective and subjective conditions favoring working-class political activity and participation in the management of the state and economy. Above all, the extent and gravity of the danger should not be denied, nor should the party succumb to the pressure of the bureaucracy, still less itself become an instrument for helping the bureaucracy to usurp power. In 1962 Fidel Castro voiced burning denunciations of the incipient bureaucracy in the Cuban workers' state and followed this by condemning the bureaucracy as being based on *materially privileged* elements in the state and the economy, divorced from the mass of workers. The attack Fidel Castro launched against the Anibal Escalantes of Cuba sounded like a repetition of Leninist and Trotskyist speeches heard in the Soviet Union almost forty years ago!

In the same way the theory of the permanent revolution, kept alive by the Fourth International as a precious heritage received from Trotsky, has been confirmed to the hilt both negatively and positively. (Negatively, by any number of defeats of the revolution and by the inability of the bourgeois leaderships in countries like India, Tunisia, Morocco, etc., to carry out a radical land reform; positively, by the fact that wherever some of the historical tasks of the bourgeois democratic revolution, above all land reform, have been carried out it has been through establishment of a workers' state, as in Yugoslavia, China, Vietnam, and Cuba.)

The Trotskyist estimate of the fundamental change in the world relationship of forces which occurred with the victory of the Chinese Revolution is today accepted by the whole international communist and revolutionary movement. The Trotskyist analysis of the class nature of the Soviet Union enabled us to foresee as early as 1946-47 that even in the countries occupied and bled white by the Soviet bureaucracy in Eastern Europe, a great upsurge of productive forces would follow the then noticeable breakdown if the structures of these countries were to be adapted to that of the Soviet Union.

The Trotskyist analysis of the world situation enabled us to foresee before Stalin's death the upsurge of the Soviet proletariat and the deepening crisis of Stalinism which would eventually head toward political revolution and the restoration of Leninist-type proletarian democracy. The Fourth International was the only tendency inside the international labor movement which, at the height of West European "prosperity" and on de Gaulle's coming to power, kept faith in the revolutionary potential of the European proletariat, thereby accurately foreseeing the new working-class struggles which in 1960 began flaring up in Belgium, Spain, Italy, and elsewhere.

If we turn from the field of *ideas* to that of *organiza-*

tion, the world Trotskyist movement appears to be far less successful. With the exception of Ceylon, the Fourth International has not yet achieved durable mass influence in any country. Its sections are still *nuclei of future mass revolutionary parties* rather than revolutionary parties in the full sense of the word; i. e., organizations able *under their own banner* to mobilize sizeable sectors of the working class.

This gap between the power and correctness of the program of Trotskyism and its weakness as an organized movement has been noted repeatedly, especially by new layers coming from large Communist parties and colonial revolutionary organizations. They incline to agree with the programmatic concepts of Trotskyism but remain skeptical about the organizational achievements and possibilities of the Trotskyist movement. The contradiction is a real one and deserves the most thoughtful consideration.

First of all, the problem must be brought into historical perspective. *The Trotskyist movement has no interests separate and apart from the long-range ones of the world proletariat.* It is not interested in constructing an "organization" simply for its own sake or as a mere pressure group. The organization it seeks to build is a definite means to a definite end — the victory of the proletariat on a world scale. This requires the highest possible consciousness, and therefore complete honesty and integrity, no matter how bitter the immediate consequences. These qualities often contradict rapid construction of an organization. The Fourth International has no choice but to follow this difficult course, for it is demanded by the interests of the world socialist revolution. Insofar as it represents the theoretical and political consciousness of that mighty process, its own ultimate fate cannot be separated from it.

To assess the strengths and weaknesses of the Fourth International in a more reasonable way, it is well to compare it with its predecessors. The First International, established under the direct leadership of Marx and Engels, never achieved great organizational strength, no matter how stupendous its theoretical accomplishments were in the history of mankind. The Second International added to the theory of Marxism and built huge organizations. But these all ended in the debacle of 1914. To achieve victory in Russia, the left wing found it necessary to split from the parent organization. The Third International moved ahead rapidly under the beneficent guidance of the Bolsheviks to succumb to Stalinism and end finally in shameful dissolution as a wartime gift from the Kremlin to Roosevelt, the political chief of Allied imperialism. Obviously it is not easy to construct a revolutionary-socialist International and bring it to successful accomplishment of its aims.

Bearing in mind the program for which the world Trotskyist movement is struggling, it is quite superficial to accuse it of organizational stagnation. It is many times stronger today than at its inception in the days of the Left Opposition in the Soviet Union or at the time of the assassination of its founder. Less than ten sections were present at the founding conference of the Fourth International in 1938; less than twenty at its Second World Congress in 1948. Today Trotskyist organizations exist in forty countries and most of these organizations are stronger than they were ten or twenty years ago — if they existed at all at that time.

Two significant developments must be stressed. In the first place the Trotskyist movement in recent years has grown in a notable way, more or less following the general rise of revolutionary developments on a world scale. This fact in itself proves that the Trotskyist movement corresponds to the *objective needs of the world proletariat* and is not a mere passing phenomenon peculiar to particular countries for a brief phase. Especially worth noting is its success as against other oppositional trends in the communist movement which began initially with much greater strength. Among these we may list the Bordigists in Italy, the Brandlerites in Germany, the Lovestonites in the United States, the Catalan Federation in Spain, the Communist League in Japan, and a number of others. All these "national communist" oppositional tendencies completely failed to develop into worldwide organizations and most of them have all but disappeared or are weaker than the Trotskyist forces even in their home base. It should be observed that one competitive oppositional trend, the Yugoslav Titoists, have held state power for nearly twenty years, and yet have proved incapable of offering a serious challenge on the international field.

Secondly, Trotskyism has again and again proved its attractiveness to revolutionary-minded youth, whether originating in the Social Democratic or Communist parties, and in countries as different as the United States and Belgium, France and Japan, Indonesia and Italy, Greece and Britain. This is striking proof that the Trotskyist movement corresponds to the burning need on an international scale felt by thousands of vanguard elements moving away from the opportunist policies of the traditional working-class leadership and seeking ways and means of building a new alternative revolutionary leadership capable of guiding mass struggles to success.

The contradiction between the correctness of the program of Trotskyism and the organizational weakness of the movement struggling for its realization is not new. In the late twenties and in the thirties it commonly took the form of the skeptical question, "If Trotsky was so right, how did he happen to lose power to Stalin and why is he unable to regain it?"

What was lost sight of in this personal symbolization of the problem was the ebb and flow of opposing social forces which Trotsky and Stalin represented. Trotsky's incapacity to hold power after 1924 was directly related to his capacity to win power in a situation like that of 1917. In remaining faithful to the long-range interests of the proletariat, Trotsky had to share its temporary eclipse in the Soviet Union under the rise of the reactionary social forces which Stalin came to represent and to express. With the downfall of the Stalin cult, Trotsky's star has again begun to rise in the Soviet Union — in other words, the proletariat there is once more beginning to move into the political arena.

In the final analysis, the fate of the Trotskyist movement is linked to the dialectical interrelationship between the three sectors of the world revolution. This is the necessary basis for any real understanding of the organizational vicissitudes of the Trotskyist movement, including solutions for its most difficult organizational problems.

Being proved theoretically correct in the twenties and thirties did not lead automatically to the strengthening of the Trotskyist movement. Trotsky's theory explained why the British general strike of 1926 was lost, why the Chinese Revolution of 1925-27 was lost, why Hitler was able to come to power virtually unopposed, why the Spanish Revolution was defeated, and why the great upsurge in the French labor movement in the middle thirties came to naught. But these defeats were defeats for the proletariat and therefore defeats for the Trotskyist movement, and it suffered the most heavily of all. Its cadres were decimated, whether through discouragement, capitulation, imprisonment, or outright murder. All world reaction centered its most terrible blows against the Trotskyist movement—from Stalin through Roosevelt to Hitler. In all history no radical political movement has suffered such persecution or received so little help from sources outside its own ranks as the Trotskyist movement. That the pioneers could hang on at all is monumental testimony to the tenacity of the human will.

With the turn of the class struggle on an international scale at the end of World War II, it might have been expected that the Trotskyist movement would be the first to profit from the new upsurge. Its interrelationship with the concrete process of world revolution proved to be more complicated than that. The Trotskyist movement could benefit only in the final analysis and in the long range.

To understand this, it is necessary to go back to the most important single event in World War II—the victory of the Soviet Union. This victory started a chain reaction, the end of which is not yet in sight. The oppressed peoples of the world turned again as they had at previous times to the first workers' state for inspiration and guidance. But government power in the Soviet Union was held by the Stalinist bureaucracy. Consequently this bureaucracy—and not Trotskyism—was temporarily strengthened.

This paradox was explained at the time by the Trotskyist movement. We also forecast that the very forces strengthening the bureaucracy would soon begin to undermine it, and the end consequence would be the doom of Stalinism. It took until 1956, however, for this process to register even partially in the official declarations of the Soviet government, and it is only today that the world monolith has been shattered irrevocably, opening the way for new political currents that tend to gravitate toward Trotskyism. The tendency can clearly be seen in the pattern of the rise of the workers' states since the end of the war — from Eastern Europe to Yugoslavia and China and finally to Cuba, the leadership has demonstrated increasing independence from the Soviet bureaucracy.

The tendency can be seen in another way. The breakup of the Stalinist monolith has been accompanied by an increasing necessity for discussion among the Communist parties, and an increasing need to deal with real issues in a reasoned way instead of in Stalin's way of substituting false issues and replacing reason by epithets, slander, and frame-ups. It is instructive for instance to see that one of the major points under worldwide debate today is the necessity of extending the proletarian revolution as the only realistic way to end the threat of imperialist war. Clearly the disputants are nearing what up to now has been considered exclusively the realm of Trotskyist discourse. The victory of the Soviet Union in the war, the victory of the Yugoslav and Chinese Revolutions and most recently the Cuban Revolution, as well as the destruction of the Stalin cult, cannot help but strengthen Trotskyism. As I.F. Stone, the astute American radical journalist, observed after a trip to Cuba, the revolutionists there are "unconscious" Trotskyists. With the coming of full consciousness among these and related currents, Trotskyism will become a powerful current.

This in turn will influence the development of the three sectors of the world revolution. The appearance of mass Trotskyist parties will bring to bear a new powerful force in the political arena. Even before these parties gain majority status in various countries, their mere presence and the partial successes they will begin to register can profoundly influence world events by hastening the natural rhythm of the revolutionary process in the three main sectors.

The cadres of the Fourth International carried out their revolutionary duty in keeping alive the program of Trotskyism and adding to it as world events dictated. But this does not signify that the organizations adhering to the program of Trotskyism were immune to the effects of long years of isolation and persecution. Two main problems have proved of perennial concern. At times a tendency has appeared here or there that sought a short cut to the establishment of a mass organization. Such experiments have in every instance proved disastrous, ending in the disappearance from the revolutionary-socialist movement of many of those who became caught up in these adventures. A greater problem has been the occasional rise of sectarian tendencies. In contrast to the opportunists, who seek escape from the pressure of the hostile environment by moving away from principles, sectarians retreat into the books and convert the texts into dogmas.

A revolutionist isolated by circumstances over which he has no control can fall into sectarianism quite unconsciously. It is therefore a more insidious danger for a small organization than opportunism, which is generally easier to recognize.

The building of an alternative leadership of the working class; i.e., of new revolutionary mass parties, remains the central task of our epoch. The problem is not that of repeating over and over again this elementary truth, but of explaining concretely how it is to be done. In fact, the building of revolutionary mass parties combines three concrete processes: the process of defending and constantly enriching the Marxist revolutionary *program;* of building, educating and hardening a revolutionary Marxist *cadre;* and of winning *mass influence* for this cadre. These three processes are dialectically intertwined. Divorced from the mass movement, a revolutionary cadre becomes a sect. Divorced from the program of revolutionary Marxism, cadres immersed in the mass movement eventually succumb to opportunism. And divorced from practical testing by cadres struggling as part and parcel of the masses, the revolutionary program itself becomes ossified and degenerates into a sterile incantation of dogmatic formulas.

The world Trotskyist movement has given much consideration to the problem of setting out with small forces to win the working class and organize it into a party capable of challenging the rule of the capitalist class. The over-all principle on which it has proceeded on the organizational level is the Leninist dictum that a revolutionist must not permit himself to be separated from his class under any circumstances. It is thus the norm for Trotskyists to belong to the union of their trade or industry and to play an active role in union affairs no matter how reactionary the union bureaucracy may be. They likewise belong to the big organizations of the masses whether they be nationalistic, cultural or political in character. Insofar as possible, they advance the ideas and program of Trotskyism among the members of these organizations and seek to recruit from them.

In countries where the masses have an old tradition of class consciousness and powerful political organizations, as in Western Europe and Australia, an especially difficult problem is posed for the revolutionary nuclei. Because of this tradition and the power of their numbers, these organizations command deep loyalty from the workers. As a result of past defeats and the long period of bureaucratic control over the labor movement, the masses, when they display readiness to take the road of revolutionary action, do not begin with a fully developed Marxist consciousness but with an outlook which is closer to left centrism.

In addition to this, the bureaucratic leaderships do not facilitate bringing revolutionary Marxist educational material to the ranks. They operate as ruthless permanent factions, completely hostile to the ideas of Trotskyism and prepared to engage in witch hunting and the use of the most undemocratic measures against those who advance fresh or challenging views.

Such are the general conditions that must be faced by the revolutionary nuclei. They have no choice but to practice "entryism"; that is, to participate as an integrated component in the internal life of the mass movement. The special function of the nuclei in such situations is to advance transitional slogans that serve to bridge the gap between the inadequate consciousness of the masses and the objective need to enter into action on the road to revolution. The revolutionary nuclei actively participate in building left-wing tendencies *capable of leading broader and broader sections of the masses into action.* Through the experiences built up in these actions, they assist in transforming the best forces of these centrist or left-centrist tendencies into genuine revolutionary Marxists.

The purpose of "entryism" is not to construct a "pressure group," as some critics have charged, but to build a mass revolutionary Marxist party in the real conditions that must be faced in a number of countries. The tactic is mined with dangers and difficulties and cannot be successfully carried out unless these are constantly borne in mind. But for a certain stage of work, no practical alternative remains open. Owing to national peculiarities, the tactic has many variants. It must be applied with great flexibility and without dogmatism of any kind. The norm for those engaging in it is to maintain a sector of open public work, including their own Trotskyist publication.

No matter what the specific situation may be in which a Trotskyist organization finds itself, so long as it remains essentially a small propaganda group, it cannot play a leading mass role. Nevertheless it can work effectively in helping the masses to learn by experience through active and persistent effort at bridging the gap between their level of understanding and the objective situation. Stated in the most general way, this is also the course that must be followed to become a mass party. It is summed up in the "Transitional Program," written by Trotsky in 1938. This program must be kept constantly up to date through study of shifts in mass consciousness and through constant effort to connect up with them.

An acute problem in relation to the construction of revolutionary-socialist parties in many countries is lack of time to organize and to gain adequate experience before the revolution breaks out. In previous decades this would signify certain defeat for the revolution. Because of a series of new factors, however, this is no longer *necessarily* the case. The example of the Soviet Union, the existence of workers' states from whom material aid can be obtained, and the relative weakening of world capitalism, have made it possible for revolutions in some instances to achieve partial successes, to reach certain plateaus (where they may rest in unstable equilibrium as in the case of Bolivia), and even to go as far as the establishment of a workers' state. Revolutionary Marxists in such countries face extremely difficult questions, from an inadequate level of socialist consciousness among the masses to a dearth of seasoned or experienced cadres to carry out a myriad of pressing tasks. No choice is open to them in such situations but to participate completely and wholeheartedly in the revolution and to build the party in the very process of the revolution itself.

The building of new mass revolutionary parties remains the central strategic task. To coordinate this work, the existing nuclei of these parties must be brought together in an international organization.

The final test of truth, as Marxists well know, is human action. Without the test of action, all theory becomes bare and sterile. The correct analysis of the world situation today is more complex than ever before. One fact alone graphically illustrates this: the peoples of more than one hundred countries are for the first time in history constantly involved in world events, sometimes in a highly explosive way. Only analysis of the world situation, constantly re-examined and tested in the light of practical action, can enable all the sectors of a worldwide movement to feel the pulse of history in the making. Only an International based on democratic centralism, permitting different tendencies to confront each other democratically while uniting them in action, can allow experiences from all corners of the world to become properly weighed and translated into revolutionary tasks on a world scale. It is not possible on the national field any longer to arrive at a correct analysis or action without a general understanding of world developments. Never have countries and national sectors of the working class been so interdependent as today. The view that revolutionary movements can be built on a "national" scale or in "regional" isolation has never been so behind the times as in the age of Intercontinental Ballistic Missiles and travel in outer space.

What is involved is the construction of something qualitatively different from the mere sum of the national organizations. By pooling national experience and opinion in accordance with the rules of democratic centralism, it is possible to build an international leadership much superior to anything within the capacity of a single section. The basic concept is not that of assembling a staff of intellectuals, however valuable and necessary this is, but of combining on an international scale leaderships that are deeply rooted in their own national soil and connected in a living way with the masses of their own country. An international leadership of that kind is capable of performing the difficult dual task of keeping theory up to date and of working out viable policies of revolutionary action on the great world issues of the day.

The necessity to build a strong, democratically centralized International is underscored all the more by the present dialectical relationship between the three main sectors of the world revolution. In the advanced countries, the International can perform crucial services in behalf of revolutions in colonial countries, opening up ways and means of appealing to the feeling of solidarity that exists even among the most politically backward workers. The International can help the fighters of the colonial revolution remain true internationalists, retaining their confidence in the world proletariat and learning to distinguish the working masses in the imperialist countries from the governments and the treacherous leaders of the traditional mass organizations. Among the advanced workers, intellectuals and youth of the workers' states, the International can play a special role in helping them to dig through the debris of forty years of falsification, distortion and slander as they seek to find their way to revolutionary Marxism.

The victory of the Cuban Revolution has led some tendencies in the international labor movement to put a question mark on the necessity of building revolutionary Marxist parties, and especially on the necessity of building a democratically centralized revolutionary Marxist International. Such a conclusion is all the more unfounded in view of the fact that Fidel Castro, as a result of his own experience in a living revolution, today stresses the decisive importance of building Marxist-Leninist parties in all countries.

In truth, the need to build revolutionary mass parties and a revolutionary-socialist International flows from the objective tasks facing the proletariat in seeking power, in winning it and in exercising it after the victory. The inadequacy and treachery of the old leaderships of the working class have made the need all the more imperative. The threat of nuclear annihilation has converted it into a matter of life and death for all mankind. There is no way to win world socialism except through revolutionary mass parties fraternally associated in an international organization. Difficult as the task may seem, it will be accomplished — and in time.

THE UNFOLDING NEW WORLD SITUATION

By Jack Barnes

The world situation now emerging is qualitatively different from that of the post-World-War-II "cold war" period.

The detente between the major workers states and world
imperialism signifies that the original post-World-War-II
"cold war" framework of international capitalist economic
and diplomatic relationships has been discarded and that
American and world capitalism have shifted their strategy
with regard to the world revolution.

The immediate postwar framework was laid out at three
gatherings:

1. In the late fall of 1944 at Bretton Woods, New
Hampshire, the American dollar was made the basis for
a new world monetary system. American imperialism's
economic supremacy among the capitalist powers enabled
it to establish the dollar as the universal equivalent in
world trade and the currency that other countries would
accept as the base of their own. The dollar was considered
to be "as good as gold" throughout the capitalist world.
But this turned out to be true only so long as American
economic supremacy was unchallenged, giving stability
to the dollar. And this didn't last as long as they hoped.

2. A little more than a year later, in Fulton, Missouri,
Winston Churchill made his "Iron Curtain" speech,
signaling the formal opening of the "cold war." The im-

perialists inaugurated the military-diplomatic policy of "containment." Their ultimate goal was to stop the extension of the world revolution, isolate the Soviet Union, and, if possible, overturn the workers states. This policy lasted almost a quarter of a century.

3. Then, one year later, at the 1947 Harvard University commencement exercises, George C. Marshall laid out the plan for reconstructing Europe on a capitalist basis, under the hegemony of an American capitalism armed with the atomic bomb. The Marshall Plan was launched with the calculated risk of reviving potential capitalist competitors in order to stave off the greater danger of socialist revolution in Europe.

These three pillars of capitalist world politics rested on the unquestioned military and economic superiority of American imperialism. Only the American colossus was in position to assume the role of world financier, world cop.

This period has now ended. The detente signals a major turn by American imperialism, a general decision by the ruling class to reorient its global strategy.

The Effects of Vietnam

Vietnam was an acid test. It laid bare the limitations faced by American imperialism in acting as world cop, maintaining a preponderant military position, keeping the international monetary system stable, and retaining world economic superiority in the context of a radical change in the political moods of the American populace itself.

The problems engendered and exacerbated by the Vietnam war made it necessary for the American imperialists to extricate themselves militarily from Vietnam, and better protect their interests vis-a-vis capitalist competitors. In so doing, they had to reorient their international strategy. A rollback of the workers states had to be deferred. What was immediately required was a detente with the USSR and China. This meant the end of Bretton Woods; it meant the end of the structure of interimperialist economic relations of the Marshall Plan and the post-Marshall-Plan era; and it meant a new stage in interimperialist competition, rivalry, and conflict, particularly over the vast potential markets in the workers states.

At home, Nixon's August 15, 1971, wage-price freeze speech signaled a new determination by the government to use its power as the executive committee of the ruling class to get greater productivity from the American workers, lower the rate of wage increases, and thus to maintain a little longer the edge in productivity it still has over Germany and Japan.

This reorientation by American imperialism does not arise from a genuine growth and economic strength relative to its competitors, but from a decline in its relative position. The political, military, and economic situation that was faced by American imperialism was becoming more and more untenable. A retreat was called for, not the initiation of a more aggressive world counterrevolutionary thrust. The attempt at establishing a new world equilibrium is designed to cut losses and regroup the still very considerable forces at the disposal of American capitalism.

The receptivity to Nixon's moves shown by Brezhnev and Mao derived not from positions of strength on their part but from positions of weakness flowing from their utopian efforts to build "socialism in one country" for a petty-bourgeois bureaucratic caste.

The contradiction between their own bureaucratic needs and the needs of the masses are particularly visible in the case of the Soviet Union and Eastern Europe, where domestic dissatisfaction and restlessness continue to mount. Brezhnev's stated goal? "Peaceful coexistence" (i.e., counterrevolutionary collaboration with imperialism) in exchange for long-term credits, equipment, and foodstuffs to help pacify their own dissatisfied masses at home.

Ten Elements of U. S. Strategy

Let us single out ten of the major elements of American imperialist strategy in the new world situation.

1. *Acceptance of the workers states as here to stay for the next historical period.*

Washington's policy is to block any extension of the

socialist revolution but to recognize that it is not now realistic to move toward a military rollback of the existing workers states. Basic parity, a "balance of terror," exists on the nuclear-military level between American capitalism and the Soviet Union.

2. *Recognition of the need for and the possibility of obtaining collaboration from the Chinese and Soviet regimes in holding back the colonial revolution, especially the tendency of national liberation struggles to develop into socialist revolutions.*

One of the big lessons the imperialists learned in Vietnam was the importance of assistance from these counter-revolutionary quarters. The collaboration of the Moscow and Peking bureaucracies became imperative to save imperialism in Vietnam, at least temporarily, in view of the economic and political situation faced by the American rulers internationally and at home. Moscow and Peking, following the Stalinist policy of peaceful coexistence, proved only too eager to render such assistance. And their assistance to imperialism will not be limited to the colonial world.

3. *Insistence that America's capitalist competitors share more of the economic and political burden of policing the world.*

Washington will still play the role of head cop, but the other capitalist powers will be called upon to take on more duties. No longer is U.S. imperialism simply going to play the role of quartermaster for junior partners. It is calling upon them to pay a larger share of the expense both directly and through trade and monetary concessions. At the same time, its nuclear arsenal puts it in a qualitatively different league from its capitalist competitors. Its nuclear capacities are only matched by those of Moscow; hence the central importance of the detente in the new international situation.

4. *The detente involves more than Washington, Moscow, and Peking. Each of U.S. capitalism's competitors is jockeying for maximum individual advantage.*

The West German ruling class has concluded "normalization" pacts with Moscow, Poland, East Germany, Czechoslovakia, and others. In fact, "stabilizing" the German question, accepting two Germanys with clear boundaries was, along with the betrayal of the Vietnamese by Moscow and Peking, one of the preconditions to the evolution of the detente.

Besides West Germany, the other Common Market countries, plus smaller capitalist powers outside of Europe, including Canada, indicated that they do not accept U. S. imperialism's acting or speaking unilaterally for them vis-a-vis the workers states or each other. The Japanese rulers rapidly drew the necessary lessons from Nixon's "surprise" trip to Peking, and opened a thaw of their own in relation to China.

Because of their qualitatively larger economies and military resources, Washington and Moscow confront each other as super powers. In this "special relationship," the detente gives the U. S. capitalists an extra edge in the competition for the Soviet market. But the "special relationship" affects and is affected by fundamental shifts in policy by the rulers of all the main capitalist powers and by the bureaucracies of the deformed workers states, each acting in its own individual interests.

5. *The dollar has been dethroned and the entire structure of world trade, upon which capitalist prosperity has depended, has been threatened.*

The difficulties of arranging a new stable international monetary system are immense. The U. S. market remains the largest by far and U. S. overseas investments and loans far outweigh all others. Thus the U. S. inflation is internationalized and the crucial question behind all currency negotiations becomes — who will pay for the inflation of the dollar?

American capitalist superiority still prevails, but now it is first among equals — equals who demand to be treated as such and who will use all the means available to them to make sure that they are. This is the result of the deepening competition.

It is in this framework that the new bargaining over trade, monetary, and military arrangements takes place. This is why the capitalist class — in Europe, more and more in the U. S., and tomorrow in Japan — must force the working class to endure more intensive exploitation to make their "own" capitalism more competitive.

6. *The Soviet Union and China are no longer viewed*

*by imperialism simply as fortresses of the class enemy
with an alien set of property relations, to be militarily
contained and rolled back. They are now considered to
be economically vulnerable, increasingly open to the penetration of capital, increased trade, and the extraction of
raw materials and energy resources — markets for which
all the capitalist powers must compete.*

Previously, partial detentes and minor experiments in
summitry were overwhelmingly political in character. As
these unfolded we contended that the economic openings
inside the Soviet bloc, in terms of markets, trade, and
concessions (eventually investment concessions and mixed
ownership), did not loom large in the considerations of
the advanced capitalist states. This is no longer the case.

The potential scope of the markets, the resources potentially available, and the willingness of the bureaucracies
to lower the barriers to the penetration of western capital
have brought about a shift in imperialist policy toward
the Soviet Union, Eastern Europe, and China under conditions of intensified monopoly competition for markets.
This makes the question of "who gets there first" — to the
markets of the workers states — a central new factor in
imperialist diplomacy.

7. *The fierce antagonisms engendered by the Sino-Soviet
dispute can become even more explosive.*

The hostility arising from the narrow conflicting national outlook of the ruling castes in Peking and Moscow has
already shown that they will resort to means verging on
war to gain national advantage. The Chinese correctly
sense the danger represented by the Brezhnev doctrine of
"limited sovereignty" and they view the threat of the Soviet
nuclear superiority in this light.

We can expect more and greater betrayals of the world
revolution by both Moscow and Peking as they vie for
the political and economic favor of world capitalism. That
is the logic of peaceful coexistence, that is the historical
logic of Stalinism.

8. *While Moscow and Peking's great betrayal has been
consummated, the civil war in Vietnam is not over. The
outcome is not definitively settled.*

The capitalist puppet regimes in Indochina are thorough-
ly corrupt and incapable of meeting the basic needs of the

workers and peasants; and the price of maintaining them in power remains high for the U. S. rulers.

The masses have not been crushed, and the class struggle continues to unfold — but within the new political framework of the detente, with the imperialists pressing from one side and Moscow and Peking from the other.

The great obstacle to the continuing class struggle achieving an early victory is the concerted pressure on Hanoi from Washington, Peking, and Moscow. The Stalinist nature of the Vietnamese leadership and its reliance upon China and the Soviet Union as its major source of material support makes it susceptible to this pressure.

9. *There is recognition of the political resistance at home to waging wars against the colonial revolution in the name of anticommunism.*

The domestic consequences of the Vietnam war among the American youth, and in the class struggle as a whole, were not anticipated by the ruling class. A repetition of such military adventures could have incalculable consequences inside the United States. The American rulers must now take into account their inability to gain popular support for such wars. This is a new historical limitation.

10. *The accords on Vietnam can prove to have a highly contradictory effect on the colonial revolution.*

A clearcut victory for the Vietnamese revolution would have enormously accelerated the revolutionary process elsewhere. Instead, the setback has served to dampen outbursts in other lands. Nevertheless, the stubborn resistance of the Vietnamese people and their capacity to force a military withdrawal of U. S. imperialism, after ousting the French troops, remains an inspiring example.

The U. S. retreat also encourages the semicolonial countries and smaller capitalist powers to engage in maneuvers aimed at winning greater elbow room. This has been especially visible in Latin America, which U. S. imperialism regards as its own backyard. These changes reflect the weakening of capitalism as a world system, one of the consequences of the intervention of U. S. imperialism in the Vietnamese civil war.

And we can add an eleventh point, which the American rulers may not see clearly enough to incorporate adequately in their strategy. While the detente may ease some of the economic pressures they and their competitors face, and result in some setbacks to the world revolution (as we have seen in Indochina), it will not guarantee maintenance of the status quo.

To the contrary, over the long run it exacerbates the already explosive contradictions not only in areas like the Arab East and the Arab-Persian Gulf — but especially in the workers states themselves. It increases the arenas of interimperialist competition and conflict.

And it plants the seeds of further upheavals in the class struggle and radicalization in the USA right in the center of this unfolding world process.

No Peace in the Class Struggle

What the detente entails, of course, is a shift in all international political relations: among the imperialist nations and blocs; between the imperialist powers and the workers states; among the workers states; between imperialism, the colonial and semicolonial countries, and the workers states.

The agreements between Washington, Moscow, and Peking are made on the basis of the current world relationship of forces; but the agreements themselves affect this relationship.

This alteration in the world political situation submits the political capacities of all the various tendencies that aspire to leadership of the working class to a major new test. Each is challenged to make a correct analysis and to arrive at the necessary political conclusions.

One of the problems in analyzing the situation is that we do not yet know the entire picture in detail. The important decisions are made in secret negotiations between representatives of top circles of the capitalist ruling class and the ruling bureaucratic castes. But while many of the agreements are hidden from the workers, enough facts do come to light to expose the broad outlines.

What both sides seek to accomplish in the detente, and a necessary ingredient of its success, is a large measure of stability, that is, class peace. But as recent events have indicated, stability and class peace are very elusive goals in this period of the decay and decline of capitalism as a world system.

The class struggle has not been halted, reversed, or annulled by Nixon, Brezhnev, and Mao; nor will it be. It continues, but within an altered set of conditions.

The problem is not the combativity or the revolutionary potential of the working class and its allies. The problem remains the crisis of proletarian leadership.

On the Economic Front

Let us now examine some of the elements of the new situation in somewhat greater detail.

First, let us consider the economic situation in the capitalist world and the growing interimperialist rivalry.

The international recession that began in 1969 eroded the relative strength of the American economy. A much deeper downturn, with a far worse outcome for the American ruling class, was averted only because the German and American recessions did not coincide. The balance-of-payments crisis grew worse and worse and international confidence in the dollar crumbled.

On August 15, 1971, Nixon launched his international economic counterattack, which included a frontal attack on the American workers. Nixon laid the groundwork for what will eventually be transformed into an "incomes policy" — to use the British term — at home. But he did so in a tentative, "phased" way, calculated to preserve the cooperation of the labor bureaucracy and avoid a massive eruption of the class struggle on the economic front.

While there was some resistance, the American workers did not respond in an explosive way. Because of this, Nixon was able to accomplish his initial goal: even with the devaluation, he was able to slow down the rate of U.S. inflation in comparison with that of competitive capitalist powers and to slow down the rate of wage increases. Despite the worsening inflationary situation in the U.S., there have been much higher rates of inflation in Europe in the last three years, and the same will be true again this year.

Nixon's economic counterattack also included a new economic offensive in relation to the Soviet bloc markets.

In this sphere for a number of years the European capitalists (and Japan to a growing extent) have developed lucrative trade relations. The so-called Eastern market has been their preserve, primarily because of the embargo or partial embargo maintained by U.S. imperialism. Nixon had to penetrate the preserve, and the machinery was set in motion with the detente. Trade concessions and growing economic relations were no longer to be solely the prize of the Germans, the Italians, the French, the British, the Belgians, the Dutch, etc. The American capitalists now enter the arena as a competitor in that field — and they aim to become the major beneficiary as rapidly as possible. They have both the economic resources — and the necessary nuclear arsenal in the closet — to strike the kind of bargain they envisage with Moscow.

During the 1969-72 world capitalist recession, the first since the post-World-War-II boom began, the rate of employment declined while inflation continued to mount — what the bourgeois economists call "stagflation." And the capitalists got off easy this time as the recessions in Germany and the USA did not have troughs simultaneously — an event which would have made the decline incalculably worse for every single advanced capitalist country. Stagflation and the threat of deeper world recession has left marks upon the consciousness of the workers.

Recently the *New York Times* reported the results of an expensive research project carried out by the University of Michigan's Institute for Social Research. The researchers discovered that "consumer attitudes changed radically during the last few months, growing more and more pessimistic as food prices kept rising . . . a substantially larger proportion of families think they are now worse off than before and furthermore, expect to be still worse off in the future. . . . Forty-four percent of those surveyed thought the rate of inflation would accelerate in the year ahead. . . . A record low eighteen percent believe there will be good times for the next five years, while half expect a recession." (April 24, 1973.)

They didn't have to spend thousands of dollars to find that out. It is obvious that there is a change in attitude among American workers. Workers are no longer confident of good times ahead; they no longer feel secure about continuing employment and wage raises adequate to maintain their living standard. There is an important change taking place in the general consciousness of the class about what the social system, the boss, and the job have to offer them in the future. And the paltry results for the workers of Nixon's first few "phases" toward an incomes policy have reinforced this change.

What is the logic of a so-called incomes policy?

First, if partially successful, it will lead to a big profits boom for the capitalists. Why? Because they are holding down wages and not prices. That is exactly what is happening now in this country. It still seems like a recession to the unemployed workers, now numbering 5 percent of the workforce. And to all of us who are eating less meat but paying more, it certainly seems less than a boom. But to the ruling class, it is one of the great profit booms in post-World-War-II history.

No capitalist regime in this epoch, not even a fascist regime, has ever been capable of stabilizing and holding down prices — even if it wanted to. The entire purpose of an "incomes policy" is to keep a lid on wages, to halt or at least to slow the rate of wage increases. The purpose is to reduce labor's share of what it produces, while productivity rises, and thus to increase the rate of profit for the capitalists.

There is a second aspect to the logic inherent in an "incomes policy." Wage controls cannot be sustained without chipping away at the rights of the working class, both its rights within the unions and eventually its democratic rights as a whole. A class that is free to organize and strike, that has the right to decide the provisions of every contract, is not going to put up with wage controls in the face of mounting inflation that reduces its standard of living. So the ruling class is impelled to first attack these rights and then — if it plans to maintain an "incomes policy" for any length of time — to attack the political rights of the workers.

What are the prospects ahead for the world capitalist economy?

While there will be ups and downs and very possibly an extended period of economic competition and diplomatic maneuvering, and perhaps even periods of relative economic prosperity for the capitalists — which is certainly one of the goals of the detente — there is no possible return to the pre-1967 period.

There is no return to the period before massive payments deficits and the fall of the mighty dollar, before the new competitive squeeze caught up with American capitalism, before the social and economic results of the Vietnam war, before the May-June 1968 events in France.

We rule out the possibility of a new interimperialist war in the period ahead. American nuclear hegemony vis-a-vis its competitors is decisive. Besides, the capitalist ruling circles are convinced that the final victor, as in World War I and World War II, would be the socialist revolution. Thus, given the current political, economic, and military situation, the capitalist rulers will try to avoid dropping the H-bomb on each other.

While excluding that possibility in the immediate future, we will certainly see a continued deepening of the rivalry, competition, and infighting among the capitalist powers — not because they want to, but because they have to. In the course of this conflict they are going to demolish some of the current mythology about their harmonious relations, the mythology that formerly surrounded institutions like NATO, the International Monetary Fund, and the Common Market. In reality the Common Market is not much more than a customs union, and not an irreversible one at that. The key is the fact that not a single one of the ruling classes is willing to surrender its national sovereignty, its ultimate reliance on state power to preserve its economic, monetary, and military interests.

We will witness a continuation of Japan's rise among the world imperialist powers. Prime Minister Tanaka, to be sure, politely met with Nixon, smiled, pledged eternal friendship, bought military hardware and commercial airplanes as he promised — but simultaneously he was preparing a trip to China to reestablish diplomatic relations. The continued economic penetration of Brazil, the competitive penetration of the Chinese and Soviet markets, and the reestablishment of the wartime "East Asian coprosperity sphere" have never ceased being goals of the Japanese ruling class.

And the goal of West German Chancellor Willie Brandt's

policy of developing openings to East Germany and Moscow is not a bid for another Nobel Prize—unless this time it's one for economic "aggression," that is, competing successfully with Nixon for the "Eastern market."

In Italy, in France, and in Britain, the resistance of the workers to the various brands of incomes policies has hindered "their" bourgeoisie's capacity to more rapidly improve their competitive stance vis-a-vis U.S. capital. And this makes Rome, Paris, and London less receptive to the attempt by the American rulers to extract concessions from them in trade, monetary adjustments, and in underwriting the costs of U.S. occupation troops as their contributions to solving Washington's problems.

We see the smaller imperialist powers frantically attempting to maneuver within this new framework. This is reflected in the rise of bourgeois nationalism in Canada and Australia. The local capitalists want to see what "independent" moves are possible in view of the weakening of Wall Street's power and standing.

We will see more of this as some of the semicolonial countries and smaller capitalist powers attempt to gain room for maneuver aimed at gaining a larger share of the pie. They will not hesitate to shift their ties and change the relations that governed their actions in the past period. Policies like those used by the regimes in Peru, Chile,* and Argentina will appear elsewhere, and the petroleum exporting countries won't be the only ones seeking to impose a better bargain.

What we are witnessing is a further confirmation of the judgment that capitalism is in its death agony. The new developments highlight the incapacity of American capitalism, the most powerful the world has ever known, to police, control, and dominate the world according to the pattern envisioned at the end of World War II. The much heralded "American century" has turned out to be somewhat shorter than one hundred years.

---

*This speech was given before the September 11, 1973, coup toppled the Allende government.

Kissinger's "Year of Europe"

This new world situation is recognized by the main sectors of the ruling class. Several days ago, on April 23 [1973], Henry Kissinger delivered a major speech calling for a new Atlantic Charter to mark "The Year of Europe."

This policy statement, reflecting the consensus of the ruling class of the United States, outlined the new relations it sought to impose upon the world. Every one of the fundamental points we have been discussing and analyzing can be noted in the speech, including the demise of the Bretton Woods agreement, the limits of military power, the costs of empire, and the new competitive situation among the capitalist states.

Within this framework, Kissinger was telling the European, Japanese, Canadian, and other capitalists what the American rulers are bidding for.

To really understand Kissinger's speech, it is necessary to translate his diplomatic language into class language. That's not really so difficult.

Kissinger began by describing the previous era as finished: "The era that was shaped by decisions of a generation ago is ending."

Here is his version of that preceding period: "In the forties and fifties the task was economic reconstruction and security against the danger of attack." In other words, the containment of the class struggle and the military preparations to roll back the workers states.

"The West responded with courage and imagination." In other words, Europe had no choice but to accept American domination; in exchange, capitalist property relations in Europe were saved by the Marshall Plan, following the Stalinist "peaceful coexistence" betrayal in 1945-47.

But, Kissinger affirms, there is a problem now. "In Europe a new generation . . . takes stability for granted." However, he continues, "it is less committed to the unity that made peace possible and to the effort required to maintain it. In the United States decades of global burdens have fostered and the frustrations of the war in Southeast Asia have accentuated a reluctance to sustain global involvements on the basis of preponderant American responsibility."

To cope with this problem he calls for "a new era of creativity in the West." And he concludes with an appeal: "We ask our friends in Europe, Canada and ultimately Japan to join us in this effort. This is what we mean by the Year of Europe."

Translated to convey the new reality, it means that given the present relationship of forces and the new economic problems, Washington's junior partners now must help foot the bill for policing the world for capitalism. For the specter of world revolution still haunts world capitalism, and the Yankee bomb is its ultimate defense. And it can't be had at wholesale prices, or without trade and monetary concessions as part of the package.

When Kissinger reaches what the bourgeois commentators call "the most diplomatic and most philosophical part" of the speech, he touches a problem of some dimension. "The political, military and economic issues in American relations," he declares, "are linked by reality, not by our choice nor for the tactical purpose of trading one off against the other. The solutions will not be worthy of the opportunity if left to technicians. They must be addressed at the highest level."

Later he returns to amplify this theme: "If [these questions] are left solely to the experts, the inevitable competitiveness of economic interests will dominate the debate. The influence of pressure groups and special interests will become pervasive. There will be no overriding sense of direction. There will be no framework for the generous solutions or mutual concessions essential to preserve a vital Atlantic partnership."

James Reston, a revolting journalistic sycophant when a policy pronouncement is handed down by the ruling class, called it "in the best sense of the expression, a 'Presidential speech,'" and summarized Kissinger's point this way: "But before these practical questions are handed over to the technicians [the cold technicians, as opposed to the "Dr. Strangelove" who delivered this address], and they begin squabbling about dollars, interest rates, tariffs, and all the other things that divide nations, maybe somebody ought to think about the political and philosophic questions that America, Europe and Japan have in common. That is what Mr. Kissinger presented to the world from the president last night." (*New York Times,* April 24, 1973.)

We think there is a slight imprecision here in the terminology. Their problem does not lie with the technicians and the experts. These are the code words for the reality as explained by Marx: the law of value, the anarchic competition of capitals for profits, and the uneven and combined development of world capitalism. It is not the technicians and the experts who create these problems. The technicians and experts simply mirror this reality as they squabble over the means to maximize profits for their respective ruling classes.

What Kissinger was really saying is: We're going to fight you on this. We're in no condition for generous solutions and we intend the "concessions" to be as one-sided as possible. The American "technicians and experts" will insist on getting trade and monetary concessions not justified in face of the declining productivity differential of American capital. They will seek to get these concessions on the basis of the size of the U. S. economy, the power of its military arsenal, and the lack of a clear alternative to the dollar as the world unit of account. That's how the "political, military and economic issues" are linked.

Kissinger goes on: "The task is all the more difficult because the lessening of tensions has given new impetus to arguments that it is safe to begin reducing forces unilaterally. And unbridled economic competition can sap the impulse for common defense. All governments of the western alliance face a major challenge in educating their peoples to the realities of security in the 1970s." Translation: You better be prepared to put even more of a squeeze on your workers to foot more of the cost of our world counterrevolutionary efforts which we intend to continue! And in the face of the unfolding detente it may not be so easy politically. You may also find in your working class a "reluctance to sustain global burdens."

To make sure no one misunderstands, Kissinger adds: "There is an increasing uneasiness — all the more insidious for rarely being made explicit—that superpower diplomacy might sacrifice the interests of traditional allies and other friends." Never, never, he assures them. But since that is just what has happened over the last two years, he should have added, "Well, hardly ever!" Underneath the appeal for understanding and collaboration is the threat of economic warfare and a new rise of protectionism in the most basic sense.

"The relaxation of tensions to which we are committed makes allied cohesion indispensable, yet more difficult." That is the other side of the detente. How willing are Nixon's competitors to pay more for policing the world when they are not sure how much they need it — especially as it will involve resources that they can use to raise productivity and compete more efficiently? And especially if there is to be no "rollback" and Brezhnev and Mao are to collaborate in restraining, containing, disciplining, and — if necessary — suppressing any revolt that threatens to upset the status quo.

The Year of Atlantic Disunity may be a more accurate title than the Year of Europe.

At the very same time as Kissinger was giving this speech, in which he talked about the need for the imperialists to collaborate on the "energy crisis," another speech was being given in Tokyo which provides an example of exactly what kind of collaboration is in store.

This speech was given by a man named Jamieson, who is the chairman of Exxon, the largest oil corporation in the world. Jamieson criticized the Japanese (without naming them) for trying to "save money and assure themselves of adequate supplies by making direct arrangements for supplies [of oil] from producing countries." He said, "There is no evidence that such supplies will be any less costly than oil obtained through the international companies."

I'm sure the applause was very polite — if somewhat restrained. The *New York Times* reporter added that among the polite applauders were representatives of the ministry of a Mr. Nakasone, who released a little information about himself and his plans the following morning to the press, which reported: "Mr. Nakasone, whose ministry oversees the oil industry [in Japan], is scheduled to leave shortly on a 10-day visit to four major Middle

Eastern oil producers — Saudi Arabia, Iran, Kuwait, and Abu Dhabi. It is reported that he will offer those nations economic aid in return for an *independent* oil supply" (*New York Times,* April 25, 1973).

So, beneath all the diplomatic language and talk about the desire for maintaining a smoothly functioning capitalist alliance are the harsh realities: deepening economic competition between the capitalist powers; the prospect of exacerbation of this competition as a result of the openings afforded by the Sino-Soviet dispute and the detente; and the determination of the American rulers, that even though they must treat other capitalist powers on a more equal footing than before, they will continue to remain on top.

Moscow and Peking as Rivals

How do the workers states fit into the overall world situation?

In recent months, Peking and Moscow have seemed to be vying with each other in putting on a craven display before the ruling classes of the major imperialist powers. This month the award probably goes to the Chinese bureaucracy, which managed to recognize Franco's Spain only one week after East Germany and before the Soviet Union, and to praise the Greek colonels for remaining independent of the "Soviet sphere of influence." But we can be sure that Brezhnev will exert every effort to regain the award when he visits Nixon.

Moscow and Peking's great betrayal of the Vietnamese in 1972 and the further unfolding of the detente confirm to the hilt what Trotsky warned of the consequences that would flow from the Stalinist theory of building "socialism in one country"; consequences which ineluctably lead to the betrayal of the world revolution.

In both the Soviet Union and China crystallized parasitic castes monopolize state power. Their fundamental concern is the maintenance and expansion of their own material privileges on the basis of nationalized property. The attitude of these castes towards the world revolution is one of total hostility. They view it as a threat to their own precarious rule. Where they are able to influence revolutionary movements, they use these movements as small change in diplomatic dealings aimed at maintaining their own positions.

There is no reason to believe that they will not go further in their betrayals or in cementing blocs and consummating deals with the bourgeois powers in their quest for advantage in their internecine struggle.

The Sino-Soviet dispute is only the sharpest reflection of the fundamentally competitive relations among privileged Stalinized bureaucracies, each of which is guided by narrow national interests.

If, as we believe, foreign policy constitutes an extension of domestic policy, it is excluded that these bureaucratic castes can adopt a policy of proletarian internationalism and of collective and collaborative development of the productive resources of the workers states. Their limited national horizons and bureaucratic rivalries and material interests preclude it.

The only way this can come about is through political revolutions that overthrow the totalitarian bureaucracies and establish workers democracy, which alone can bring about genuine internationalism in foreign policy, including complementary economic planning among the workers states, and a concerted effort to extend the world revolution. Those who think this necessity has been eliminated by Soviet economic growth are even more mistaken than Bukharin and Stalin were in 1928. The Soviet Union today is more dependent on the world market and world resources, not less.

The Soviet Union has massed divisions of troops and nuclear arms on its border with China. The propaganda emanating from Moscow is blatantly racist, loaded with "yellow-peril" appeals. In Eastern Europe, with the Soviet invasion of Czechoslovakia in 1968 came the formal announcement of the Brezhnev doctrine of limited sovereignty, which proclaims Moscow's right and duty to suppress not only any popular uprising but any fundamental policy alterations in the deformed workers states that threatens the stability of the rule of the Soviet bureaucracy.

The Chinese bureaucracy, in turn, has shown in action how counterrevolutionary its foreign policy is. Since the detente we have seen its pro-NATO statements, its encouragement of the NATO nations not to withdraw a single division from the western boundaries of the Soviet Union, its expression of anxiety lest Greece fall into the Soviet sphere of influence, since the colonels, as Peking sees it, are a lesser evil. This is but an extension of the game of power politics that found crass expression earlier in the betrayals of liberation struggles in Bangladesh, Sri Lanka, and the Sudan.

As the ramifications of the broad detente continue to unfold, we will see more and more evidence of the kind Trotsky pointed to when he explained that the Comintern and all its parties have become instruments for upholding the bourgeois order on a world scale. And we will see deepgoing effects as the Communist parties whose basic policy is determined by their subordination to the bureaucracies in Moscow or Peking try to rationalize and apply the new twists and turns made necessary by the new "peaceful coexistence" detente.

We noted also that the detente underscores our analysis of the Stalinist character of the Chinese regime and of the Chinese Communist Party. At the end of 1968, when so few commentators and "experts" believed it, Joe Hansen wrote in *Intercontinental Press* that the Chinese were offering a peaceful coexistence deal to the Nixon administration. Actually, they were proposing anew a deal that had been offered before—immediately after World War II, and right at the time of the conquest of power.

Joe Hansen said that this time the deal might well be accepted, and that if so, it would mean the betrayal of the Vietnamese and lead to a very different world situation. If the deal should materialize, he added, it would surprise "more than a few observers of the Chinese scene." In the July 26, 1971, issue of *Intercontinental Press* Joe Hansen was able to reprint this article without changing a word. As he said in a short editorial note, "Although it was written before Nixon was sworn into office as president, the article makes timely reading in connection with the current turn in diplomatic relations between Peking and Washington."

The immediate reason for the detente was Nixon's need

for assistance in salvaging the Vietnam situation for imperialism. And there was only one place he could turn for help.

Nixon was in trouble! There was no possibility of convincing the American people to acquiesce in a further deepening of the war. The detente coincided with the magnificent spring offensive — possibly the military high point of the national liberation struggle. That's when Nixon felt compelled to turn to Moscow and Peking for help. There is no question that history would have been changed by the mass antiwar reaction here if Moscow and Peking had stood up to Nixon's new bombing and mining offensive.

Within the context of the detente and the deepening of the Sino-Soviet dispute there will be more room for maneuver for the Eastern European rulers, and this will coincide with the growing insecurity of their rule as the detente raises the expectations of the workers and intellectuals in all the workers states. But this will all take place in the framework of the Brezhnev doctrine of limited sovereignty. That's an explosive scenario.

Mao's ideologists have now begun redefining all of the East European countries as no longer fascist but once again socialist countries so it can initiate relations with them without "ideological" embarrassment. Rumania, for example, has once again become a socialist country, in Peking parlance.

The papers published a fascinating feature by David Rockefeller, who visited Moscow and the countries of Eastern Europe for the Chase-Manhattan Bank at the opening of the detente. He told how, as he hit each new capital, his hosts had already heard about the tempting offers of concessions, trade, financial needs, etc., that had been listed by the government officials in the previous country. Each new capital seemed to be eager to slightly outbid the previous one. He thought this augured well for his bank (and class).

The *immediate* goal of the capitalist rulers is not to reverse the conquests of October 1917 through economic penetration, although economic penetration will assist in achieving that long-range goal. The immediate economic goal is to penetrate the Soviet, East European, and Chinese markets in a new way to help solve the deepening economic problems that the capitalist powers face in this period of imperialism's decline.

The longer-run significance of this detente and the accompanying economic penetration of the workers states by Western capital will touch off growing debate in the workers movement.

We will see renewal of the argument over the class character of the workers states. What criteria are to be used to determine their character as workers states? What changes are necessary to alter our characterization? What is wrong with Moscow and Peking's analysis of each other? Can there be a "cold" social counterrevolution in the workers states? All these questions will be raised again.

The Colonial Revolution

In general, the intensification of interimperialist competition for control of world markets exacerbates the need to control the sources and drive down the prices of agricultural and industrial raw materials. This will add to the fuel that has kept the fires of colonial revolutions permanently burning since World War II.

One has only to look at the struggles in each of the Portuguese colonies in Africa, the ferment in Zimbabwe (Rhodesia), the new Black proletarian upsurge in South Africa — not to speak of the Palestinian liberation struggle, the revolution in Bangladesh, and the war in Vietnam itself — to be reminded that the "powder kegs" of imperialism that Trotsky pointed to in 1928 are still exploding and will continue to do so.

It is also likely that there will be more room for maneuver by the indigenous ruling classes in the colonial world under these new circumstances, especially in some of the larger and more advanced semicolonial countries, like Brazil and Argentina. American capitalism will meet with sharper competition from Europe and Japan — a development welcomed by the Argentine bourgeoisie and the Campora regime,* for instance.

---

*Hector Campora was elected president of Argentina in May

There have also been cases in which rival imperialist powers have seized on colonial struggles to advance their own interests on the battlefield, most notably the Congolese events in the first part of the 1960s and the Nigeria-Biafra war. Coupled with this is the process of developing "client states," like Brazil and Iran, which are expected to take on the role of military surrogates for U. S. capitalism in protecting imperialist interests on the regional level.

Furthermore, Washington seeks to utilize the detente with Moscow to preserve the "status quo" in the Arab East and around the Arab-Persian Gulf in favor of Israel and Iran and against the Arab revolution. Protection of U. S. oil "rights" there takes on increasing importance under the pressure of intensified world competition.

But none of these measures resolves the native bourgeoisie's fundamental incapacity to meet the most pressing needs of the masses or to play a genuinely independent role in the international political, economic, and military arena. The new world political situation changes nothing regarding the incapacity of the comprador and national bourgeoisie to solve historical problems that only the working class can solve today.

In all probability, we will see a continuing trend towards the classical pattern of class struggle in the colonial world, that is, towards further confrontations between the massive and growing urban proletariat of the major colonial and semicolonial countries and their ruling classes and the bourgeois state. The trend along this line in the past three years does not constitute an anomaly, but is the pattern for the future.

Of course, there can be no universal model to be emulated everywhere. It would be fatal to make the same mistake that OLAS [Organization of Latin American Solidarity] made in seeing guerrilla war as the only possible model for the Latin American countries. But we believe it is clear that the general tendency is toward more classical methods of struggle, towards the use of methods traditionally employed by the urban proletariat.

1973 as a stand-in candidate for Juan Peron, who was not allowed to run. He then resigned, however, to enable Peron to run on his own, and Peron was elected president in September 1973.

As in Chile, the workers and their allies in Argentina have been on the offensive. They can win significant concessions from their ruling class, including greater democratic rights on the political arena, opening up a period of relatively favorable conditions to carry on the class struggle.

We will see more bourgeois regimes, like the one in Peru, seeking to take advantage of some of the weaknesses of world capitalism to solve their problems — the way Cardenas tried to solve them in Mexico and the way Nasser tried to solve them in Egypt. There will be growing competition to pluck the ripe plum of Brazil, where the Japanese capitalists have already made one of their greatest coups.

The students will continue to play a very important role in the colonial world — witness, for example, the recent student actions in the Arab East and in South Africa.

None of the problems of the colonial world can be solved by petty-bourgeois nationalist leaderships, by guerrilla warfare, or by some new gimmick that has not been thought of before. To the degree that Trotskyist parties are not constructed in these countries all evidence confirms that the Stalinists and Social Democrats will be able to reassert themselves. There can be no automatic bypassing of these bureaucratic misleaders in the labor movement. The experience of Chile, Argentina, and Peru, among others, drives this point home anew.

Interrelation of the Three Sectors of the World Revolution

Within this new world situation, we also can anticipate more complex relations among the three sectors of the world revolution. There is likely to be much more interpenetration of ideas, models, conflicts, and the emulation of examples.

It is evident that the national question will be a major and permanent factor in the class struggle, not only in the colonial world, but in the advanced capitalist countries and in the degenerated and deformed workers states where national oppression is an acute issue.

The influence of the youth radicalization and the resurgence of the student movement in the advanced capitalist countries may be asserted more rapidly than ever before in the Soviet bloc in the years ahead. Movements like the struggle for women's liberation can affect the consciousness of the masses of the world more quickly than before.

The new rise of workers struggles in Western Europe can have the kind of effect in Poland, for example, that was not before possible — and vice-versa. But as the detente unfolds there will be increasing interpenetration and a new richness of relations between the radicalization that is continuing in the advanced capitalist countries and the reawakening of the workers, students, intellectuals, and their allies in the Soviet bloc.

Bringing Our World View Up to Date

In 1963 the Socialist Workers Party drew up a document of political principles that was adopted as the basis for reunifying the then-divided world Trotskyist movement: *For Early Reunification of the World Trotskyist Movement.* That statement has met the test of time. It remains a solid, principled groundwork for world Trotskyism. But important new phenomena have occurred, and embryonic developments which were only noted in that document have matured. These have to be taken into consideration in bringing that document up-to-date. We plan to do this in cooperation with comrades around the world.

In that project, special note must be taken of the following nine points:

1. *The rise of the youth radicalization, its international impact, and its historic importance.*

There is evidence that another wave of student and youth upsurge has begun. We've seen new student upsurges in South Africa, Morocco, and Egypt. We've seen the first confrontations by the students with the colonels' regime in Greece. The Spanish students helped to spark the big new wave of workers' demonstrations. There was the massive student upsurge in Belgium. And in France, in the last month, there has been the biggest upsurge since May-June 1968; in many ways, the student pro-

tests there were more advanced than the student component of the May-June 1968 general strikes.

This phenomenon of the youth radicalization and our
analysis of it must be brought up-to-date on the basis
of the resolution adopted unanimously in 1969 by the
United Secretariat of the Fourth International, entitled
*The Worldwide Youth Radicalization and the Tasks of
the Fourth International.* *

2. *The national question.*

We have always ascribed great importance to the national question in the colonial world. But we must also
take note of its growing importance in the advanced capitalist countries and the workers states.

This question will not disappear or drop to a subordinate or peripheral character. On the contrary. The Irish
question, for instance, is one of the keys to the crisis
of British capitalism. The Quebec question will certainly
play more than a modest role in the Canadian revolution.
The Ukrainian question, as Trotsky predicted, will never
allow the overlords in Moscow to rule in peace.

3. *New features of the political revolution.*

This will include the rise, scope, and limits of the coura-
geois intellectual opposition in the Soviet Union; the lessons of the Czechoslovak and Polish events; the lessons
of the Cultural Revolution and the evolution of Chinese
Stalinism; the problems of workers self-management. Under this point, of course, we must note the further evolution of the Sino-Soviet dispute with its threat of military
conflict.

4. *The decline of the relative stability and growth of
world capitalism that marked the 1950s and the early
1960s.*

We must take note of the new stage that has been reached
in the evolution of imperialism and the new problems
world capitalism faces that are leading to new outbreaks
of class conflict. We must outline the fundamental turn
in world politics rooted in this "new" economic epoch,

---

* Reprinted under the title *A Strategy for Revolutionary Youth*
in *The Transitional Program for Socialist Revolution* (Pathfinder Press, 1973), pp. 181-203.

which so clearly spotlights the "old" contradictions outlined by Lenin.

5. *The evolution of the colonial revolution.*

Here we will have to note not only its continuing capacity to rebound from defeats (the strength, courage, and resilience of the colonial masses have been proved over and over in the last decade); we will also have to point out the limits of the petty-bourgeois leaderships that have held sway in the colonial world up until now and how the strategy of guerrilla war proved to be no substitute for the role played by a revolutionary party.

6. *The rise of the women's liberation movement and its effect on all facets of the class struggle and in all sectors of the world revolution.*

The international phenomenon of the growing radicalization and politicalization of women struggling for their economic, social, and sexual liberation is a new indication of the depth of the crisis of world imperialism. Striking at the patriarchal family system, one of the pillars of class rule, this struggle is an integral part of the social revolution. The significance of the rise of women's liberation, its importance for the revolutionary movement must be dealt with.

7. *The fundamental conclusions that must be drawn from the Vietnam experience, one of the turning points of world history.*

The strength of the national liberation struggle; and the fundamental obstacle that the program of "socialism in one country" is to its victorious culmination; the limits of American imperialism, at home and abroad; and the role of Soviet, Chinese, and Vietnamese Stalinism must be assessed.

8. *The changes that have occurred inside American capitalism.*

The new problems that the American capitalists face at home; the main features of the evolving radicalization, its potential for deepening, its contradictions, and its significance in world politics today and for the coming world socialist revolution must be indicated.

The document must take note of the difficulties facing the American ruling class in view of the current mili-

tary, economic, diplomatic, and domestic political relations that have developed; the American ruling class,
for all its power, does not have the capacity to grant
the improvement in the quality of life necessary to contain and decisively roll back the radicalization that has
begun.

9. *The fundamentally new stage of the class struggle
in capitalist Europe.*

There is a new stage in the crisis of leadership of the
European proletariat, and the European workers face a
situation today different from that of either 1963 or 1968.

These are the major developments that must be considered in a concentrated programmatic way. They show
how dramatically the class struggle has evolved since
1963.

The Continuing Crisis of
Proletarian Leadership

We will also have to draw up a balance sheet of the
continuing crisis of world leadership of the proletariat:
the Maoist Stalinist leadership, the Moscow Stalinist leadership, the guerrillaist leadership of OLAS, the petty-bourgeois nationalist leaderships of the Nasserist type, and
of course, the balance sheet on the progress and problems
of the world party of socialist revolution, the Fourth
International.

Nixon contends that we are heading into a period of
peaceful coexistence in the world. To the degree that there
are problems, he thinks, they are going to come from the
little fellows and (with Brezhnev and Mao's collaborative acquiescence) he will be able to whip them into line
pretty easily.

The whole perspective includes extended class peace at
home. Nixon may see a few potential trouble spots ahead,
but he is sure that with the help of "reasonable" gentle-
men like Secretary of Labor Peter Brennan and United
Steel Workers President I.W. Abel, the ruling class will
gain needed time to restore its rightful place in the world.
With reasonableness and collaboration on both sides at

home and abroad, he mistakenly assumes stability will be readily attained.

In the coming period, those heading up the regimes of the Soviet Union and China, the heads of the big Communist and Social-Democratic parties in Asia, Europe, and Latin America, or the bureaucratic misleaders of American labor will try to turn the detente to account in advancing their own interests. We should have no illusions about that.

The American labor bureaucrats have their class-collaborationist and narrowly nationalist answer to the problems American labor faces. Their answer is protectionism, business unionism, reliance on political "friends" in public office, cannibal unionism, increased lobbying, union officials in government posts, and long-term no-strike agreements. All the incapacities and criminal inclinations of these rotten layers will be exposed.

But Nixon fails to take into account certain pitfalls. The very steps the capitalists must take to try to get themselves out of the historical contradictions in which they find themselves will demolish the national and international class peace they seek to establish.

The most elusive culprit remains the built-in contradictions of the capitalist system. That is one "subversive" they can never put in jail.

There will be no lack of revolutionary upheavals. What is posed for us is the same question that has been central for our epoch: the question of leadership.

Our problem still remains the same as stated by Trotsky in the first sentence in the Transitional Program. "The world political situation as a whole is chiefly characterized by a historical crisis of the leadership of the proletariat." *

A new generation is now coming to understand more concretely what that statement implies. The absence of a world Leninist leadership weighs heavily as the class struggle heats up, as new sectors of the class struggle come into play, as upsurges occur in one country after another, as the masses continue to show their revolutionary capacities and combativity.

---

*The Transitional Program for Socialist Revolution, p. 72.

The acuteness of the crisis of leadership is perhaps clearer today than ever before. The lack of a Leninist party constitutes the greatest single obstacle to the victory of the world revolution.

The various alternatives to Leninism, to Trotskyism, have long demonstrated their bankruptcy. The pro-Moscow Stalinists, the Social Democrats, the labor bureaucrats, have all continued their course of betrayal.

But what of the various new alternatives that have arisen since World War II? The Yugoslav Stalinists at first purported to offer an internationalist alternative to Stalin and the Cominform* — they ended up trying futilely to realign the neutrals and politically they are clearly bankrupt. Peking proved bankrupt time and again — first at the 1955 Bandung conference with the "neutral" capitalist countries, then in trying to rally the anti-Moscow, pro-Maoist Stalinists where it could find them. Now Peking vies with Moscow for the favor of American imperialism.

The Castroists, to their everlasting credit, bypassed the Stalinists and established the first workers state in our hemisphere. But they too have been unequal to the responsibilities of international leadership, although they did try to extend the revolution by consistently urging and aiding emulation of their guerrillaist line. They set up OLAS, carrying their line to the world leadership level as best they could. They tested their guerrillaist line in practice; it was found wanting. The guerrilla strategy advanced by Castroism became one of the obstacles in the fight for the construction of a revolutionary leadership.

The Nasserists and other petty-bourgeois nationalists — and the new lefts in various countries, who never got off the ground — all have been found wanting.

---

*The Communist International (Comintern) was disbanded in 1943 as Stalin's gift to his wartime allies. When the "cold war" deepened, however, Stalin established a new international organization of Communist parties in 1947 called the Communist Information Bureau or Cominform. It was dissolved in 1956.

How Trotskyists Can Go Wrong

But also found wanting in this period since World War II are various tendencies that began as Trotskyists, that began as Fourth Internationalists, that attempted to offer alternatives but rejected our method — the Leninist strategy of party building and the method of the Transitional Program. Two of the clearest examples are to be seen in the courses followed by Gerry Healy and Michel Pablo and their followers.*

Healy and Pablo were both capable and talented revolutionists. Both began as Trotskyists, with origins in a common tradition, as part of a common world movement. Yet the roads they took have led into dead ends. Why?

We have to examine the reasons very carefully; and our answer will be political, because it is not primarily a matter of ill will or personal deficiencies. We have to describe where and how Trotskyists can go wrong; it is the only way to avoid repeating the errors.

The answer lies not in the specific and limited experiences in their countries, although there is no question that this played a role. Healy was shaped by British politics and was marked by the weaknesses of British radicalism, particularly its provincial outlook. Pablo was politically shaped first in Greece, then in France, and was marked by the one-sidedness of many European Marxists. But these are not fundamental factors. They affect all revolutionists.

---

*Michel Pablo attended the 1938 founding congress of the Fourth International and was a leader of it in the 1940s and 1950s. He led the International Secretariat during the split in the Fourth International, but left the International in 1965, two years after the reunification.

Gerry Healy was the leader of the British section of the Fourth International at the time of the split. His organization was part of the International Committee during the split, but opposed and did not take part in the 1963 reunification. By the time of reunification, Healy's group, the Socialist Labour League (later renamed the Workers Revolutionary Party), had developed in a sectarian direction.

No, different experiences are not the primary thing, although one must be conscious of them. One must not explain away false ideas but rebut them.

More than anything else, the dead ends that Healy and Pablo came to stemmed from misreading the lessons of the world revolution since World War II; from failing to measure up to the complicated theoretical, political, and organizational challenges that were put to our movement in that quarter of a century.

They were unable to analyze to the bottom the gigantic historical detour that occurred as a result of the strengthening of world Stalinism at the end of the war. They were unable to understand the contradictory character of this phenomenon; they failed to see how petty-bourgeois parties, including Stalinist parties, for the first time in history could stand at the head of revolutions that led to the establishment of workers states, but at the same time could not become, in a historical sense, a substitute for the Leninist party on a world scale as well as in their own countries.

They failed to comprehend fully the obstacle that Stalinism represents to the world revolution and the complex and unanticipated theoretical and political problems posed by these postwar developments. They were unable to apply the Leninist strategy of party building and the method of the Transitional Program in the face of these new contradictory phenomena.

One error to avoid is that of the simplistic school that says: they led a revolution so they can't be Stalinists. An example of this error, one of the most tragic, was that of Arne Swabeck in the SWP.*

A nimber of others internationally followed Pablo. Some of the original Pabloites carried this line to its logical conclusion by joining the Stalinist parties, not as a deepentry tactic, but as neo-Stalinists: George Clarke's colleagues, Michelle Mestre and John Lawrence, for example. # They redefined Stalinism; but Stalinism had not redefined

---

*Arne Swabeck was a founder of the American Communist Party and of the Trotskyist movement. He was a leader of the Socialist Workers Party until the 1960s when he became a Maoist. Swabeck left the SWP in 1967.

George Clarke was a leading supporter of Pablo in the SWP.

itself. It had not become an "adequate instrument" for advancing the class struggle.

There is also the danger of falling into the obverse error, that of the school that says: they were petty-bourgeois or Stalinists, therefore the revolution did not occur.

Healy provides a prime example of this error. He could not recognize the stages in the evolution of the government and state that the Cuban revolution established. Nor could he recognize its class character. He also failed to pass one of the central tests posed to revolutionists: recognizing a revolutionary development when one occurs and identifying with it. Understanding the class character of the Cuban state was a precondition to correct analysis of its development.

This error has a lot in common with Stalinophobia, which fails to identify with and orient to the revolutionary masses in motion for fear of contamination from the Stalinists who may, under certain circumstances, stand at the head of these masses.

In the postwar years, we have seen some tendencies bypass Stalinism and register important achievements. The great example was the revolutionary team around Castro and Guevara. They bypassed the Stalinists and led the peasants and workers to the establishment of a workers state.

But even bypassing and negating Stalinism at one stage of the revolution, up to and including the establishment of a workers state, does not solve the historical question of proletarian leadership. It merely poses the next question: the theory, organization, and leadership necessary to extend and deepen that revolution, which is ultimately the only way to defend it.

It is important to recognize that the Chinese experience,

Expelled from the SWP, Clarke attended Pablo's Fourth World Congress but walked out after his motion that the Fourth International disband was rejected.

Michelle Mestre and John Lawrence were leading supporters of Michel Pablo in the French and British sections respectively. Soon after the International Secretariat's Fourth World Congress in 1954, both left the Trotskyist movement to join the Communist parties in their countries.

the Yugoslav and Vietnamese experiences, and the Cuban experience occurred as detours — not new historical norms — for the world revolution. To fail to understand this point ultimately means to adapt to non-Leninist currents — as Pablo adapted to Stalinism, as whole sections of the American and European left adapted to Maoism and Castroism. And the logic of adaptation is to lose our most precious assets: clarity on principles, the transitional approach, and the strategy of constructing a Leninist party. No one can build the Leninist party but convinced Leninists, and no other instrument is adequate to the job we have set for ourselves.

It is wrong to see Leninism, as Pablo did, as a broad general category covering the organization of revolution in our epoch, including of course the theory of the organization of the revolutionary combat party, but including it only as one variant among others. It is wrong to say that wherever the proletariat has won a victory or even a partial victory in the absence of a Leninist party this calls for redefining Leninism.

It is wrong to conceive of Leninism as a general framework that can encompass the various radicalized leftwing forces and the various "far-left" ideologies that can arise in this epoch. This approach rejects what is unique about the Leninist vanguard — the principled clarity and programmatic norms needed to construct the kind of party that places the proletariat itself in the leadership of the world revolution.

The logic of this error leads to dispersing the Leninist organization into some other "vanguard." It leads to a search for substitutes for the Leninist party. This false concept always comes down to one simple idea: other forces are bigger, they are heading or have headed revolutionary upsurges, they may not be as pure as we are, but they are an adequate tool. That was Pablo's fundamental mistake. It meant a fundamental break with our traditions and theory of party building, a fundamental break with Leninism.

There is no vanguard that is adequate other than the Leninist vanguard. There is no way to construct a Leninist party other than through participation in the class struggle by the nuclei of conscious Leninists. The Stalinists of whatever variety, the guerrillaists, and the petty-bourgeois nationalists constitute obstacles on the path to the world revolution; they are obstacles to advancing the new working-class upsurges in Asia, Africa, Latin America, Europe, and North America. They offer only a dead end.

You know, we have always disagreed with Isaac Deutscher's choice of titles for his trilogy — *The Prophet Armed, The Prophet Unarmed,* and *The Prophet Outcast.* Describing Trotsky as a prophet shows the limits of Deutscher, but it doesn't tell us the truth about Trotsky. Trotsky was not a prophet. Trotsky was a revolutionary scientist. He was not a prophet who had a vision around which he constructed a schema to guide his action. That is a form of idealism, a form of impressionism, that leads to adaptationism and it is alien to Trotskyism. No, Trotsky wasn't a prophet. He was a scientist who dissected the living class struggle on the basis of the principles around which a Leninist party must be built to lead the class struggle forward.

We reject all the false answers, from Stalinism and Social Democracy to every other non-Leninist variant that has arisen in the postwar period.

We must continue to build Leninist parties on the basis of the method outlined in the Transitional Program adopted by the founding conference of the Fourth International in 1938, which was a continuation and extension of a century of Marxist analysis and practice. We reaffirmed that programmatic view in 1963 and continue to reaffirm it today.

Our view, from the very beginning, has been that the duty of the Fourth International is to be clear on this question above all else.

We fight to maintain the established Leninist norms of party building.

We view the construction of Leninist parties not as a preferable method but as the necessary method to lead the workers to victory and to guarantee that victory. That is the road we are determined to follow.

THE WORLD POLITICAL SITUATION
AND THE IMMEDIATE TASKS
OF THE FOURTH INTERNATIONAL

I. Chief Features of the
World Political Situation

"The world political situation as a whole," Trotsky wrote
in 1938, "is chiefly characterized by a historical crisis
of the leadership of the proletariat." (*The Death Agony
of Capitalism and the Tasks of the Fourth International.*)
Despite the immense developments since then, Trotsky's
judgment still remains valid. In fact the historical crisis
of proletarian leadership has grown in acuteness over
the years. Today the fate of humanity hinges on resolving that crisis in relatively short order.

1. The Ripeness of Objective Conditions

The economic prerequisites for the proletarian revolution were fully met by the turn of the century. World
War I came as a warning to humanity of the costliness
of delaying that revolution. Further major warnings in
the twenties and thirties came in the form of economic
convulsions of unprecedented depth and scope, resulting
in periodic mass unemployment and sustained pressure
on the standard of living of the masses.

Through huge expenditures in reconstructing Europe
and Japan after World War II, through increasing government intervention in the economy, and through war bud-
gets of astronomical size, the capitalist ruling class man-

aged for a period to stave off acute economic crises. The overhead cost, however, has been an ever worsening long-range inflation and an accumulation of stresses that have been building toward an acute economic convulsion. The premonitory signs include, among other things, the successive international monetary crises of the past few years and the increasing sharpness of economic rivalries.

One of the clearest indications of the trend of modern capitalism has been the erosion of bourgeois democracy on a world scale. Between the first and second world wars, European capitalism, the most highly developed and cultured sector, gave rise to fascism, the most malignant form of government in history. Fascism has continued to serve dictatorial regimes of various kinds on all continents as a model of ruthlessness and brutality.

The barbarous potentialities of capitalism were given another test run in a second world war, which far exceeded the first in destructiveness and bloodshed. The igniting of atomic bombs over two teeming population centers in Japan served as a harbinger of what is in store if capitalism is permitted to continue until it reaches the stage of a third world war. The hydrogen bomb today stands like a specter over world affairs, the latest reminder being the nuclear alert called by Nixon during the October 1973 conflict in the Mideast.

A fitting index of the degeneration of capitalism is the heightening of "gunboat diplomacy" to such a point that the Pentagon's bombing of Vietnam exceeded in destructive force the total exploded in all theaters in the six years of World War II.

Another telling index of the regressiveness fostered by capitalism is the use of torture as a systematic weapon of control. Almost half the world's governments have adopted it, and it is rapidly spreading, according to a survey made public by Amnesty International in November 1973.

The productive capacities of the world capitalist economy have undeniably grown in absolute figures compared with selected dates such as 1913 or 1939. The statistics are misleading, however, because of what is left out of account. The growth has been highly uneven. In some countries, particularly in the colonial and semicolonial sphere, economic growth has not even kept abreast of expansion in the population. So far as per capita figures are concerned, this means an absolute decline. Moreover, in some countries, particularly those whose relation to the world market has fostered a monoculture, the economies are subject to abrupt and highly dislocating turns. Still more significantly, all such comparisons leave out of account the immense losses and setbacks suffered because of depressions, wars, and preparations for new wars, not to mention the artificial level of scarcity brought about by chaining production to profit requirements and to the limitations of national boundaries.

A more realistic appreciation of how much capitalist productive relations stand in the way of optimum development of the capacities of modern industry can be gained by studying the swift rise of the Soviet Union and that of poorer countries, particularly China, where capitalist property relations have been superseded by planned production. Even though the parasitism of a bureaucratic caste has constituted a heavy and unnecessary burden, the experience of these countries testifies to the vast inherent powers of a nationalized and planned economy. It can no longer be honestly denied that economic planning on a world scale could provide abundance for all in a relatively short period.

2. Stage of Sudden Breakdowns

While technological improvements in the capitalist countries like automation and computerization have reached such a degree as to warrant, in the opinion of some, the label of "new industrial revolution," they have served on another level to deepen and extend the already existing contradictions of the capitalist system.

This has been shown with remarkable clarity in the "energy crisis." The developing shortage was noted some years ago. A direct consequence of monopolistic policies followed by the oil cartels, it reflected on a deeper level the chaos of capitalism as a whole. A relatively small withdrawal of oil from the world market in October 1973 was sufficient to precipitate an acute crisis.

In Japan, which in the capitalist sphere stands next to

the United States in productivity and which is the world's leading importer of oil, the pinch on oil supplies from the Middle East led in December to a declaration of a "state of emergency," and a government order to cut back oil and electric power to major industries by 20 percent.

In Japanese government circles, the imposition of economic controls like those in force before and during World War II were under consideration. This would mean rationing oil and all products affected by the oil shortage, the setting of production quotas, the enforcement of import and export restrictions, the imposition of foreign-exchange controls; and, of course, wage "controls."

Japan's export schedules were upset, including essential supplies to other countries in the Far East. Exports to the United States faced an uncertain future because of the rise in costs. Not only were forecasts on profits hastily revised downward, the yen itself was permitted to slump as an emergency step.

In Britain, Heath utilized the energy crisis to issue a decree in December imposing a three-day workweek on most industries. This meant pay cuts for millions of workers, a sharp rise in unemployment, widespread dislocations, and new hardships for the masses. The Conservative government took this "austerity" move after having already decreed a "state of emergency" in November in face of acute pressure for wage increases from more than six million workers. The consequence was a social crisis of unusual severity.

Elsewhere in Western Europe, the sudden oil crisis led to restrictions of varying degree in all countries, some of them reminiscent of the controls of World War II.

In the United States, the stock market dipped erratically. A "voluntary" stage of rationing of oil products and electric power was decreed while more rigorous measures were prepared.

The Common Market administration warned of a possible decline of 2 to 3 percent in gross output of goods and services in the Common Market countries in 1974 that could plunge Europe into its deepest recession since the late forties.

As the Keynesians cast about for new stopgap measures, Wall Street prognosticators speculated about the effect of the energy crisis on the already noted signs of an approaching recession that could coincide in Western Europe, the United States, and Japan.

Along with the increased possibilities of a recession, the energy crisis was immediately followed by a new inflationary leap. In 1970 Mideast oil stood at $1.80 a barrel. In January 1973 it had risen to $2.59. By December 1973 this price had quadrupled to $11.65. In other areas the giant cartels jacked up oil prices still higher. In a chain reaction on a world scale, prices on innumerable commodities skyrocketed within weeks.

In the colonial and semicolonial world, the inflationary consequences of the oil crisis promise to be particularly severe. While those countries possessing extensive oil fields stand to gain temporarily from the price increases, others heavily dependent on oil imports (India, Brazil, etc.) are placed under heavy strain. Countries not so reliant on oil because of lack of industrial development can be hard hit indirectly.

The price hikes announced by the shah in behalf of the Mideast oil-producing governments were engineered by the Aramco combine— Exxon, Mobil, Standard of California, and Texaco. The move was part of a gigantic scheme to escalate profits in oil and related industries to unheard of levels, to repeal the minimum antipollution measures that have recently begun to be placed on the legislative books in response to public pressure, to do away with safety measures in the coal mines so as to lower production costs, to remove all restraints on strip mining and exploitation of oil-bearing beds of shale, step up the construction of deep ports required for unloading giant tankers, slow down construction of new refineries, rush the construction of hazardous nuclear-powered plants to generate electricity, and squeeze out the independents in the retail marketing of oil products.

The energy crisis was utilized as an excuse by the oil barons and their governmental representatives to deal heavy blows against the ecology movement, an outstanding example being stampeding the U.S. Congress to approve construction of a pipeline across Alaska that can destroy the ecological balance of much of the remaining wilderness there.

Other consequences were to be noted. The predominance of the United States in the world capitalist system received fresh confirmation. Especially striking was the vulnerability of Japan, whose industries are heavily dependent on distant sources of oil dominated by cartels under Washington's control (or, more accurately, that control Washington). The relative weakness and disunity of the West European powers was likewise highlighted. Through the oil cartels, the United States dealt some stinging slaps to its junior partners. An indicator of this was a relative strengthening of the dollar.

The energy crisis is but a single example of what is happening to the world capitalist system. The beef shortages in the United States and Argentina should be recalled, as should the sudden power brownouts and blackouts, the disruption of telephone services, and deterioration of postal systems in various countries. Other shortages or malfunctions are impending that can lead to acute crises. In the United States, for instance, a metals shortage may be next on the list. The colonial world can be hit by a shortage in chemical fertilizers. In Tokyo and other industrial centers pollution levels are dangerously high.

The sudden breakdowns now characteristic of capitalism testify to the deepening anarchy of the system and the need for restructuring the world's economy on rational lines.

The reverberations of the energy crisis can be cited to show how timely the Transitional Program, proposed by Trotsky in 1938, has become. In the United States the proof was rather dramatic. Within days after the reduction in oil shipments was announced, various circles, despite the well-known political backwardness of the country, were demanding that *the books of the oil monopolies be opened and their profits, production statistics, and secret dealings be made public* so that appropriate action could be taken.

These are progressive demands that should be supported by revolutionists everywhere. They point quite logically to further demands, one of which was soon being advanced in the United States: *Convert the oil industry into a public utility.*

Slogans along this line, of a more and more revolutionary character, can be expected to appear as the energy crisis deepens. Exemplary ones include: *Operate the oil companies under control of the workers instead of the stockholders. Expropriate the oil cartels. Let's plan rational use of energy resources on a world scale.*

The cost to the proletariat of the energy crisis was visible almost immediately in the form of layoffs and reduced employment— on a national scale in Britain with Heath's three-day workweek. The scourge of unemployment was added to that of rampant inflation. The consequence is to be seen in a rise of mass discontent in the main industrial countries. Pressure is already developing, especially in the unions, for remedial action.

The Trotskyist movement has long advocated *a sliding scale of wages* to meet the rising cost of living. Its correlative, *a sliding scale of hours* to meet unemployment, is now becoming timely.

The struggle for such demands, involving the immediate economic situation facing workers, combines logically with the struggle for control, management, and ownership of the oil industry (and related key industries). Out of this line of struggle can emerge a revolutionary challenge to the capitalist parties, the capitalist government, and the capitalist state.

How to advance this challenge is a tactical matter dependent on the level of political consciousness of the masses and the concrete circumstances in each country, particularly the acuteness of the struggle. Sections of the Fourth International should have no difficulty in working out this problem by utilizing the method outlined by Trotsky in *The Death Agony of Capitalism and the Tasks of the Fourth International.*

The energy crisis, it should be stressed, is but a single striking current example of what is happening within the capitalist system — its growing susceptibility to sudden shocks and breakdowns — and of the new openings that are appearing for initiatives in action to be urged for adoption by the labor movement.

The energy crisis has pointed up in the most emphatic way two basic features of capitalism today: its highly integrated international structure and its imperviousness to rational planning.

The "options" chosen by the capitalists in situations

like the energy crisis invariably amount in the final analysis to merely tightening their rule and compelling the masses — sometimes with a few passing sops — to carry additional burdens. The capitalist class is adamant on retaining power and maintaining the status quo even if the end result is a new dark age or nuclear annihilation.

The masses, however, are growing increasingly dissatisfied. They are no longer inclined to passively accept the dismal perspectives offered by capitalism. Their fears have been heightened by the course followed by the capitalist rulers in the past half century; while their expectations have been aroused by what is manifestly possible through transcending capitalism and establishing an economic order based on modern science, technology, and industry. Moreover, they have seen that it is possible to break out of the capitalist system and go forward. Highly convincing demonstrations of this have taken place in Russia, China, Eastern Europe, North Korea, North Vietnam, and Cuba.

The combination among the masses generally of heightened expectations, discontent with things as they are, and awareness of the possibility of going beyond capitalism constitutes one of the chief features of the world political situation today. What the masses do not yet see clearly is the correct path to take. They are still far from having resolved the crisis of proletarian leadership.

II. The World Revolution Resumes Its Main Course

The problem of wresting power from the bourgeoisie was solved in theory at the beginning of this century by two invaluable contributions to Marxism — Lenin's plan for the construction of a vanguard party and Trotsky's theory of the permanent revolution. More importantly, as World War I drew to a close, the Bolshevik team they led in Russia solved it practically. The exemplary action of the Bolsheviks still constitutes the best and most enlightening model for study and emulation by revolutionists everywhere.

Lenin's strategy, to which he finally won Trotsky in 1917, was to build a mass revolutionary party capable of providing leadership in every area of the class struggle and organizing the struggle for power. The party provided leadership for the proletariat which in turn provided leadership for the oppressed layers in both the cities and the countryside, including the oppressed nationalities, and the peasantry — the most massive oppressed class force in the Russian empire. With the construction of a party shaped in accordance with Lenin's formula, that is, a revolutionary staff and thousands of experienced cadres bound together by democratic centralism, the workers after toppling Czarism succeeded in conquering supremacy and initiating the world socialist revolution.

Trotsky was the guiding political genius in the military field who assured victory in the armed struggle, not only in the Petrograd insurrection of October 1917 but in the subsequent civil war in which the domestic counterrevolution was backed by expeditionary forces supplied by the Allies, including the United States.

Lenin and Trotsky sought to teach the international

proletariat that the main secret to the victory of the Russian revolution — certainly the most significant event in twentieth-century history — was *political* in nature; it was the construction in time of a revolutionary proletarian party. They launched the Third International in 1919 to promote this task on a world scale.

There was no lack of revolutionary opportunities in the twenties and thirties. Europe was shaken again and again. The Chinese revolution had excellent chances of success in 1925-27.

All of these chances were missed or fumbled by failure to absorb the chief lesson of the victory of the Russian revolution and to apply it in time — construction of a revolutionary party. The principal reason for this default, after the collapse of the Social Democracy, was the rise of a reactionary bureaucratic caste in the Soviet Union, owing to the isolation of the Russian revolution, the wearing away of the generation that had made the revolution, and the general poverty and cultural backwardness of peasant Russia. Stalin emerged as the chief political representative of the ruling bureaucracy. With the death of Lenin, the Leninists soon found themselves in a minority in the Bolshevik party they had created. Those who did not capitulate were eventually eliminated, losing their lives, along with countless others, in the great purges of the thirties.

The most pernicious consequence of these internal Soviet developments was the disorientation of the proletarian vanguard in other countries. Unable to follow or understand the significance of the political struggle in the Soviet Union, the majority took Stalin to be the legitimate representative of revolutionary Marxism and the continuator of Leninism, as claimed by the Soviet government. *Stalinism* — whether in its ultraleft or rightist expressions — thus gained sway over millions of revolutionary-minded workers. Many who were repelled by Stalinism turned back toward the Social Democratic parties, giving these formations fresh vitality after the low state into which they had fallen because of their counterrevolutionary role during World War I and its aftermath. The *class-collaborationist* policies of both the Stalinist and Social Democratic parties, reaching a peak in the ill-fated "people's fronts" of the mid-thirties, doomed the spontaneous mass mobilizations of the workers and their allies that could have toppled European capitalism in those days, given the guidance of revolutionary parties constructed in the Leninist way.

The exemplary action of the Bolsheviks in solving the crisis of leadership became more and more blurred in the minds of the working-class vanguard. The lessons were kept alive only by the small band of continuators of Leninism who stood with Trotsky against the stream and founded the Fourth International on the eve of World War II.

1. The Long Detour

The immense betrayal of the working class committed by the Stalinized Communist parties cost humanity a second world war, drenching Europe, North Africa, and the Far East with blood, and setting back civilization by decades.

The United States gained preeminence among the imperialist powers. As a consequence of the destructive means taken to achieve this, however, world capitalism itself became so weakened, particularly in the German and Japanese sectors, as to permit the Soviet Union — thanks to the fundamental achievements of the October revolution — to emerge victorious, if badly damaged, despite the counter-revolutionary policies of Stalinism that had paved the way for the German imperialist invasion of the first workers state.

The dual outcome of World War II — the American predominance over a weakened world capitalism on the one hand and the Soviet victory on the other — coupled with the profoundly unsettling effect of the war on a global scale, set the main political framework internationally for the subsequent quarter of a century.

At the close of World War II in 1945, the pundits of American imperialism envisioned a "Pax Americana" — an empire of greater power and stability than anything seen since the days of Rome. Holding a monopoly of the atomic bomb, with both Western Europe and Japan lying in ruins and the Soviet Union devastated by the conflict with Germany, the rulers of the United States set their sights on "finishing the job" by bringing China under the American empire, carrying the Stars and Stripes across Eastern Europe to the Pacific, and opening up these vast regions to the penetration of capital. The first phase of this operation was the "cold war" with Truman's atomic-bomb diplomacy and stated aim of "containing" and "rolling back" communism.

Inside the United States this policy led to McCarthyism, which was given its initial impulse in 1947 under Truman.

Several unexpected developments cut across the early realization of these ambitious plans. First of all, the American troops in Europe and the Far East refused to stay abroad. Spontaneous mobilizations involving contingents on a mass scale testified to the disintegration of these forces as an instrument of imperialist policy. The demand of the GIs to return home had to be granted and new armies had to be constructed to replace them. The most propitious time for striking was thus lost.

In addition, spontaneous upsurges of the masses in Western Europe (Italy and France above all) demonstrated the precariousness of capitalism in that key area. Time had to be taken by American imperialism to shore up capitalism there, this being done under the Marshall Plan.

Although the Stalinist parties played a decisive role through their class-collaborationist policies in betraying the first great postwar opportunities for socialist revolution in Western Europe from Greece to Belgium, they could not contain the colossal upsurge in the colonial sphere that proved decisive in setting back the U.S. imperialist timetable for world conquest.

A breathing space was granted to the Soviet Union that was turned to good account. To the astonishment and chagrin of the Pentagon, Soviet scientists broke the American monopoly of nuclear weapons, exploding an atomic bomb in 1949 and a hydrogen bomb in 1953.

Moreover, in the countries of Eastern Europe occupied by Soviet troops, Stalin in reply to the cold-war offensive carried out a series of overturns of capitalism that further strengthened the Soviet Union, thus indirectly giving another impulse to the revolutionary aspirations of the masses, especially in the colonial and semicolonial areas. Like the "patriotic war" conducted by the Kremlin against the German invaders, the overturns in Eastern Europe demonstrated that at times a bureaucratic caste, in defending or advancing its own interests, is impelled to undertake actions that run against its overall counterrevolutionary policies and have objectively revolutionary consequences.

The masses of China moved into the political arena by the tens of millions. Under the exceptional conditions provided by the invasion of Japanese imperialism and World War II, and under a spontaneous mass upsurge seldom if ever matched in history in its elemental force, the peasant armies that arose in a striking parallel to the ancient revolutionary pattern in China were able to defeat the reactionary forces headed by Chiang Kai-shek and bring the Maoist leadership to power. For a while, the new regime — a workers and farmers government of a type first foreseen by the Bolsheviks in 1922 — sought to maintain capitalist relations under the formula of a "bloc of four classes." However, when it was compelled to mobilize in self-defense against the American imperialist intervention in Korea and the drive of General MacArthur's armies toward the border of China, the Maoist regime broke up China's capitalist economic structure, replacing it with a planned economy patterned after the Stalinist model in the Soviet Union.

This was an immense blow to the world capitalist system. It served to inspire hundreds of millions of the oppressed in all continents, and this effect was deepened as the standard of living of the masses in China rose swiftly in contrast to the abysmal level in India, a comparable country where the capitalist system and landlordism remained intact.

However, the peculiar pattern of the Chinese events was taken as a model by many revolutionists, who sought to transfer it to countries where conditions bore little resemblance to those in China. Guerrilla warfare in particular, instead of being taken as a tactic that had to be viewed in subordination to the key task of constructing a revolutionary party, was elevated to a strategy. It was thought that this strategy, with variations necessitated by the local terrain, could be applied universally.

It is, of course, true that in countries having a large peasant population the appearance of guerrilla contingents is often a sign of a rising revolutionary ferment. Lenin noted the spontaneous development of guerrilla warfare in Czarist Russia at the time of the 1905 revolution and sought to take advantage of it — rather unsuccessfully as Trotsky observed in summing up the experience.

Guerrilla war, expanding into a so-called people's war, likewise played a role in the Vietnamese revolution. It also appeared in a positive way as an outgrowth of the mass peasant struggle in Peru under the leadership of Hugo Blanco. It is going on in the struggles against the Portuguese in Black Africa. It may appear again in the course of revolutionary developments in some countries, particularly where guerrillas have long been endemic.

In Cuba, the Castro team scored a brilliant success by relying on guerrilla warfare to open the struggle against Batista. The victory of the first socialist revolution in the Western Hemisphere greatly reinforced the appeal of guerrilla warfare as a strategy, especially in Latin America.

The victory of the Cuban revolution in 1959 marked the high point in the influence of the Chinese pattern. On a deeper level, the particular course of the Cuban revolution resulted from the default of Stalinism and its disorientation of the workers movement, which imposed a prolonged delay in the revolution. Had it not been for the role of the Cuban Communist party in fostering class collaborationism under Batista, and had a genuine mass Leninist party existed, the Cuban revolution could have been achieved in the mid-thirties.

The victory in 1959 also marked the beginning of something new. The Cuban leaders were not of the Stalinist school — many of them were consciously anti-Stalinist. Although they were of petty-bourgeois origin, the Castro-Guevara team outflanked Stalinism from the left, opening a new phase in resolving the world crisis of proletarian leadership despite the fact that they themselves faltered in this task and eventually gave it up.

In the beginning, the Cubans undertook exemplary measures. Defying pressure from the imperialist giant only ninety miles away, they mobilized the masses and established a workers and farmers government, began a deep-going agrarian reform, and dismantled the key sectors of the capitalist structure. Proceeding further, they set up a monopoly of foreign trade and initiated economic planning. With the establishment of a workers state, they undertook a whole series of progressive measures that included eliminating mass unemployment, racial discrimination, illiteracy, and other perennial social scourges. They launched an ambitious program of building low-rent housing. They gave an immediate lift to the standard of living of the masses, and, still more significantly, opened up completely new long-range perspectives for the masses, including a comprehensive educational system.

Small wonder that the Cuban revolution gave enormous impetus to movements with similar emancipatory goals throughout the colonial world.

In the imperialist countries, including the United States, the Cuban revolution caught the imagination of hundreds of thousands of young persons, particularly the student youth, and was instrumental in bringing many of them toward revolutionary Marxism.

In Latin America an entire generation of revolutionary-minded militants devoted themselves to preparing for guerrilla war and engaging in it under the conviction that it had proved to be a surefire shortcut to victory or the only alternative to parliamentarism. The acceptance of guerrilla warfare in Latin America was not attributable to its greater applicability in this region in contrast to countries in Africa, the Middle East, or Southeast Asia, but to the direct inspiration and impact of the Cuban revolution. At the same time the consistent advocates of guerrilla warfare as a strategy could hardly confine its use to Latin America and had logically to consider and to urge its use in other areas in opposition to the methods of Leninism.

Of all the many ventures in guerrilla warfare throughout Latin America following the Cuban revolution, not a single one has led to success. The roster of those who tried it includes top-rated experts: Uceda de la Puente in Peru, Carlos Marighela in Brazil, Yon Sosa in Guatemala, and Che Guevara himself in Bolivia, not to mention dozens of less publicized figures who devoted intensive study and practice to the strategy.

A major element in their failures was the improvement

in counterstrategy developed by imperialism, and the ability of the Pentagon to deploy substantial forces under its guidance in the arena of struggle.

Another element was misjudgment of the political situation. In China a mighty revolution poured human resources on an immense scale into the peasant armies and their guerrilla adjuncts. In Latin America the theoreticians and practitioners of guerrilla warfare put things upside down. It was their conviction that the mere appearance of determined guerrillas could prove sufficient to set a human tide rolling like the one that finally toppled capitalism in China, or if not a movement on that scale then at least one comparable to that of the Cuban revolution. Consequently miniscule groups, completely isolated from the masses, engaged in operations that were put down with relative ease by the bourgeois armed forces and their imperialist backers, a conspicuous example being the guerrilla front opened by Guevara in Bolivia.

2. The Turn in the Pattern of Revolution and the New Upsurge of Workers Struggles

Unperceived by the guerrilla groups, a deep going change in mood was taking place among the masses by the mid-sixties in many parts of the world, including the areas where the guerrillas sought to set up fronts. Whereas in China, because of the exceptional circumstances mentioned above, the peasantry had taken the lead through its armies (the Maoists even put down working-class actions upon entering the cities), in Latin America the peasant struggle temporarily subsided while the urban masses began to move forward.

This shift was evidenced in a highly dramatic form in the spontaneous mass uprising in Santo Domingo in 1965. In a few days, the urban masses seized control of the city, won over part of the army, distributed arms on a broad scale, and opened a mass armed struggle that had good chances of success. It took massive intervention by U.S. troops, coupled with the absence of a seasoned revolutionary leadership, to contain and then crush the insurrection.

The Santo Domingo uprising signaled what was happening on a broad scale in the colonial and semicolonial countries having a large peasant population — the city was reasserting its political hegemony over the country-side, the proletariat was again coming into position to press its claim to leadership. The long detour away from the main road of the world revolution in the aftermath of World War II was coming to an end.

In Bolivia, one of the reasons for Guevara's lack of success in setting up a guerrilla front was his expectation that the peasants would respond to his initiative. But the pattern of revolution Guevara had in mind did not correspond to the reality. The peasants did not respond, nor did they respond to the actions of the Peredo brothers and others who sought to continue what Guevara had begun. On the other hand, in the great Bolivian social and political crises of the following years, the workers in La Paz, along with the miners, traditionally the backbone of the proletarian revolution in Bolivia, played a major role in battling the reaction and seeking to move forward.

In Chile, which moved into the political forefront in Latin America with the victory of the Allende government in 1970, the city clearly outweighed the countryside, the workers of Santiago in particular mobilizing again and again, a fact that could have assured victory had a revolutionary party existed.

Even in China a certain increase in the weight of the urban centers was observable during the "cultural revolution." This was particularly clear in the case of Shanghai at the end of 1966 and beginning of 1967 when the workers, raising a series of demands aimed at improving their standard of living, moved into action against the local bureaucracy.

The shift in focus toward the urban centers was paralleled by a rise in militancy of the workers in the imperialist sector. In their interplay, the two developments tended to reinforce each other on an international scale.

This was apparent in the giant student demonstrations in Mexico City in July-October 1968, which frightened the Mexican bourgeoisie into savage reprisals. It was to be seen in the great wave of demonstrations in Argentina in May 1969 that were touched off by the students in Corrientes and Rosario and that developed into successive urban explosions initiated by militant layers of the working class in Córdoba, Mendoza, etc. And it was visible in the strike struggles and student demonstrations that broke out in 1972 and 1973 in South Africa.

In France the rise in militancy took explosive form in 1968 when a student rebellion in Paris detonated a nation-wide general strike involving ten to fifteen million workers. The absence of a mass revolutionary party prevented the general strike from following its logical course to the establishment of a workers government; and the Stalinists and Social Democrats were once again able to save the situation for the French bourgeoisie. May-June 1968 thus entered history as a rehearsal instead of the actual opening of the socialist revolution in France.

Aside from the dramatic demonstration of the rise of working-class militancy and the importance of the youth radicalization, the May-June 1968 events revealed that the control of the class-collaborationist labor bureaucracies over the workers in Western Europe had become eroded. This was a consequence of the wear and tear suffered by the Stalinist and Social Democratic bureaucratic machines coupled with the increasing tendency of the workers to move into action under pressure from the deepening contradictions of capitalism and its incapacity to grant them long-lasting concessions.

The new rise of the class struggle in Western Europe was soon confirmed by the "creeping May" that plunged Italy into a prerevolutionary situation in the fall of 1969.

As the upsurge of workers combativity in France and Italy continued, marked by numerous strike actions, the Spanish proletariat in 1970 also began to move. Mass mobilizations, nationally coordinated by the clandestine Comisiones Obreras, protested the Burgos trial of the Basque nationalists and the victimization of other political prisoners. The years 1971-73 saw a series of militant strikes — Madrid construction workers, SEAT, El Ferrol, Bessos, Pamplona — actions that tended to grow over into even broader mobilizations against the Francoist dictatorship, challenging the Spanish rulers on a level not seen since the crushing defeat of the Spanish proletariat in the 1930s.

In Britain the mobilizations against the Industrial Relations Act, the occupation of the Upper Clydeside shipyards, and the militant strikes by the miners and dockers were all steps in a sharpening of social tensions and deepening confrontation between labor and the British ruling class that reached a new level at the end of 1973.

The rise was also reflected in the new stage of the Irish struggle. Mass mobilizations occurred in Derry in October 1968 and January 1969.

In North America, the deepening struggle in Québec expressed itself through giant nationalist demonstrations in 1968-71; and through the continual rise of labor militancy over the past decade. The April-May 1972 upsurge in Québec, initiated by a general strike of public-service employees, was the most important working-class battle in North America in many years.

Inside the United States, besides the rise of the antiwar movement, the struggle for Black liberation erupted in the proletarian ghettos of the big cities in elemental social explosions, the first one of spectacular proportions occurring in the Watts section of Los Angeles in 1965.

In Latin America, as the focus of the class struggle shifted more and more obviously to the cities, the guerrilla strategists likewise shifted, abandoning their efforts to establish military bases in the countryside. In place of this orientation, they initiated "urban guerrilla warfare." The most prominent exponents of this new line were the Tupamaros in Uruguay and the left-wing Peronists and the PRT-ERP in Argentina.

Like the practitioners of rural guerrilla warfare, the urban guerrilla groups have displayed a fatal inability to grasp the role of a Bolshevik-type party implanted in the masses. Consequently they see no need to build one. Some of them openly reject it, although it is doubtful whether they know what they are rejecting, being unable to distinguish between Stalinism and Leninism. They substitute their own action for that of the toiling masses and therefore stand apart from the struggle of the masses, which remains terra incognita to them. They reduce armed struggle to the caricature of small groups engaging in "expropriations," kidnappings, and other terroristic actions that may win them applause but not leadership of the masses.

The rising temperature and increasing extent of the

mass struggle in the cities has tended to further isolate the guerrilla groups. As this process continues to develop, more serious contenders for political leadership will come to the fore. In the long run these will prove to be the ones willing and able to learn from the example given by Lenin and Trotsky, particularly how to use the transitional method to build a revolutionary party of the masses.

The Fourth International does not reject guerrilla warfare under all circumstances. It views the utilization of guerrilla warfare as a tactical question to be weighed in the light of concrete situations that may arise in the course of struggle. What the Fourth International does oppose under all circumstances is the view that a small group can bypass the arduous task of constructing a Leninist-type party by substituting for the masses in armed struggle.

While rejecting the concept of guerrilla warfare as a panacea or a shortcut to power, the Fourth International recognizes the courage and dedication of guerrillas who stake their lives in such operations. Against the blows directed against them by reactionaries of all stripes, the Fourth International expresses its solidarity with the guerrilla fighters. Nonetheless it criticizes their course of action as politically mistaken and urges them to give deeper study and consideration to the Leninist-Trotskyist way of engaging in the revolutionary struggle for workers power.

Above all, the Fourth International calls attention to the turn in the pattern of the world revolution. Today the urban masses, with their own forms of struggle and class organization, are moving to the center of the stage.

As the proletariat again asserts its leading role in the international class struggle in a direct way, the revolutionary process will advance qualitatively. In the cities, the poverty-stricken layers of the populace, including oppressed minorities, will rally to the side of the proletariat; and the entire movement will become a powerful pole of attraction to the masses in the countryside, a phenomenon long ago anticipated by Trotsky in his theory of permanent revolution.

In colonial and semicolonial countries where the agrarian question remains acute, the inevitable new upsurges of the peasantry will add fresh dynamism to the revolutionary process. As in the Russian revolution, the proletariat and the peasantry in the coming period will tend to act in *combination* under the leadership of the proletariat (unlike the case of China, for example, in the 1940s).

Thus the turn in the pattern of the world revolution clearly signals the opening of a period in which it will become possible for revolutionary-Marxist nuclei to gain mass bases at an accelerated rate, in that way moving into position to supply the element of political consciousness required to resolve the historical crisis in proletarian leadership.

3. Interplay of Victories and Defeats in the Three Sectors of the World Revolution

The interplay of developments in the three sectors of the world revolution in the past decade has been extraordinarily clear.

On the walls of the Sorbonne in imperialist France during the stirring events of May-June 1968, the most prominent portraits were those of Che Guevara, Mao Tsetung, Ho Chi Minh, and Leon Trotsky. While the selection of these particular portraits reflected the views of contending political currents among the radicalizing students in Paris, they also indicated a common motivation, "Let's make the revolution!"

The example of the French students and that of the French working class in the great general strike touched off by the rebellion in the universities served in turn to inspire the students and workers in other lands, an outstanding instance being the student demonstrations in Mexico City in 1968.

A current example of this interplay came in the closing months of 1973. Through giant rallies and marches involving crowds of more than 100,000 persons, the Bangkok students, backed by the workers, brought down a hated military regime in Thailand October 14. Within four weeks, on the opposite side of the globe in Athens, student demonstrations backed by workers scored a partial victory by bringing down Papadopoulos, the leading figure of the military dictatorship in Greece. Among the slogans shouted by the Athenian students, a favorite one was "Thailand!"

As for the Soviet bloc, the Prague Spring in 1968 was in part inspired by the example of the Vietnamese in resisting the U.S. imperialist invasion and by the example of the student antiwar protests and demonstrations in Western Europe and the United States.

In the imperialist centers, the Algerian and Cuban revolutions played a big role in helping to radicalize the youth, particularly in France, the United States, and Canada. The Chinese revolution played a similar role in many countries. The Russian revolution of 1917 had an effect in both the colonial world and the imperialist centers that has not yet been paralleled and that still remains fresh in the minds of older revolutionists.

Within the Soviet Union today, victories of the colonial peoples, setbacks to imperialism, and the radicalization in the West serve alike to feed the fires of rebellion against the bureaucracy. On the other hand, the reports filtering out of the Soviet Union of courageous defiance of the bureaucrats and their political police by intransigent fighters for proletarian democracy help encourage revolutionists in both colonial and imperialist countries to fight more energetically against capitalist oppression.

The current rise of workers struggles in Western Europe is bound to encourage similar trends elsewhere. One of the zones where this influence can have an early effect because of its proximity is Eastern Europe. The countries there, intended by Stalin to serve as buffers against military invasions from the capitalist West, have already shown how readily they can become converted into transmission belts of revolutionary ferment directed against the bureaucratic ruling caste in the Soviet Union. An impressive example of this was the rebellion of the Polish workers at the end of 1970 and beginning of 1971 that brought down Gomulka, inspiring political dissidents in the Soviet Union and frightening the Kremlin.

While counterrevolutionary capitalist ideology may follow this path of entry to a certain degree, experience has shown that the buffer zone has much greater affinity for revolutionary ideology and for revolutionary examples emanating from the oppressed layers in the capitalist countries. It is this, and not the influence of bourgeois "life-styles" or of "hippie culture," that worries the Kremlin's watchdogs. Their own life-style is bourgeois to the core, as they show before television cameras whenever they hold a summit conference with imperialist statesmen like Nixon and Kissinger. The top Kremlin bureaucrats are themselves the most important generators of bourgeois influence in the Soviet Union. That is one more reason why they must be removed by the Soviet workers.

Also to be taken into account are defeats to the world revolution. Some revolutionary Marxists do not like to analyze defeats. They prefer to concentrate on victories — which are preferable from the viewpoint of recruiting. But defeats are of decided importance in learning how to avoid repeating errors and in determining what tasks to undertake. Defeats are likewise important because of the repercussions that must be taken into account. They directly set back the revolutionary cause in the sector in which they occur, and they act as depressants in other sectors.

The series of defeats suffered in Latin America because of reliance on the guerrilla strategy had a decided effect on world events. One of the reasons for the confidence of the Pentagon in plunging into Indochina was its conviction that it had mastered an effective "counterinsurgency" technique. As defeat after defeat occurred in Latin America, enthusiasm over the Cuban revolution waned elsewhere, quite visibly in the United States and also in the Soviet bloc countries.

The effect of two bitter defeats suffered in Brazil in 1964 and Indonesia in 1965 can be judged by considering how victories in those countries would have exhilarated the masses internationally and given mighty impulses to the world revolution.

The defeat in 1960 of the movement headed by Patrice Lumumba in the Congo not only threw back the African liberation movement as a whole, it was keenly felt in the Black liberation struggle in the United States. In the final analysis, the assassination of Malcolm X in New York in 1965 hurt the struggle in Africa.

The downfall of the Ben Bella regime in Algeria in 1965 likewise served as a source of discouragement to revolutionists throughout the Arab countries and elsewhere. Instead of another Cuban revolution lighting up the Maghreb and areas far beyond the Mediterranean, the Algerian revolution went into eclipse.

The signing of the Paris accords in 1973 represented a setback to the Vietnamese revolution. Although Washington did not realize its full goal of smashing the Vietnamese revolution and had to withdraw its troops, it remained in a relatively favorable position to preserve a capitalist South Vietnam. Instead of being able to point to a clear-cut success, revolutionists had to face up to the unfavorable aspects of the cease-fire that Hanoi was forced to accept. This task was made more difficult because the leading figures of the North Vietnamese government hailed the ambiguous compromise as an unalloyed victory.

The recent defeat in Chile was immediately interpreted by counterrevolutionary forces in neighboring countries as strengthening their hand. It cast a visible pall among vanguard elements in the imperialist sectors who were confronted with the need to organize elementary acts of solidarity with the victims of the junta instead of riding the wave of a great new victory with all the favorable consequences this would have had in their own countries.

In the Arab East the rise of the Palestinian resistance helped offset the effects of the 1967 defeat and fostered a revival of the Arab revolution as a whole. This development suffered severe setbacks in the September 1970 civil war in Jordan and later in Lebanon and other countries. As the considerably weakened Palestinian resistance organizations shifted to the right politically, individual terrorism gained headway out of desperation.

These reversals facilitated attempts of the bourgeois Arab regimes to reach a settlement with the Israeli settler-colonial state at the expense of the Palestinian people. The mounting pressure from the Arab masses to end the continued Israeli occupation of Arab lands, coupled with the beginnings of a revival of the mass movement in Egypt, led in October 1973 to the renewal of war. While the political purpose of the war, from the point of view of the Egyptian and Syrian regimes, was to head off the mass movement and gain a better bargaining position for a settlement with Israel, and while the favorable showing of the Arab armies gave these regimes an enhanced prestige, the war also fostered a vastly increased feeling of confidence among the Arab masses, which will redound in the last analysis to the advantage of the Arab revolution.

The interplay of victories and defeats among the three sectors shows how important it is to watch for the possible effect of events in one sector upon happenings in the other two. Besides paying close attention to this aspect, revolutionists must do their utmost to see that accurate information about events is gathered and passed from one sector to another. The importance of the revolutionary press appears in a new light when viewed from this angle.

Even more, everything said and done by revolutionists must be weighed not only for the possible consequences in a given country but also for their possible repercussions in other areas. Revolutionists bear an *international responsibility* for their course in the national arena.

For the Fourth International, which has sections and sympathizing groups all around the world, this has a special meaning.

As a class whose destiny it is to take human society beyond capitalism to the worldwide planned economic structure of socialism, the workers have interests that can properly be appreciated, defended, and represented only on an international level, that is, as a whole. The working class requires an international consciousness.

Without for a moment losing sight of the fact that the proletarian revolution moves along the spiral of separate countries in taking state power, the vanguard must insert the particularities of this struggle into their overall sweep and global interrelations. For this, a staff of cadres is needed — a world party of the socialist revolution.

This party, which the components of the Fourth International have sought to build for thirty-five years, follows and seeks to influence the interplay of trends in all three sectors. The analyses, proposals, and actions of the Fourth International register the advancing level of political consciousness achieved by the international proletarian vanguard. In this respect they constitute essential contributions to resolving the crisis of proletarian leadership on a world scale.

III. Radicalization and Mobilization of the Allies of the Proletariat

To break out of the decaying capitalist economic and social framework and move toward socialism, the proletariat requires the assistance of various allies. In the countryside, these include the lower layers of the peasantry; in the towns and cities, the students, artisans, members of the professions, small shopkeepers, etc. It is a problem of class leadership to break the grip of the bourgeoisie on these sectors and win them to the cause of socialism.

In the epoch of the death agony of capitalism, as is well-known, the millions of persons standing between the two basic classes can be hard hit economically — sufficiently so to cause them to begin of their own volition to seek a radical way out. Unless the proletariat offers effective leadership in time, opening up a realistic short-term perspective of establishing socialism, these natural allies of the working class can become demoralized. Out of frustration and desperation, they then become prey to fascist demagogues, as was tragically demonstrated in Italy, Germany, and elsewhere following World War I.

Since experiencing the realities of fascism in Europe, the petty bourgeoisie as a whole has tended to resist the appeals of reactionary demagogues. In this respect, the present situation is more favorable than that of the twenties and thirties. Nonetheless, with the passage of time and successsion of generations, the historic memory of the experience with fascism has grown dim. Moreover, fascism is quite capable of putting on new masks that make it more difficult to identify. Consequently it would be a grave error to count on the relatively more favorable attitude of the petty bourgeoisie as a whole remaining a permanent feature of world politics.

An ominous sign was the success of the counterrevolution

in Chile in gaining a following among the truckers, some of the university students, and petty-bourgeois housewives in the cities as the generals prepared the coup d'etat that toppled the Allende government. The Social Democrats and Stalinists in Chile closed their eyes to the significance of this growing reactionary trend among sectors of the petty bourgeoisie. They failed to grasp that their own heads were at stake. Their course led to a heavy defeat for the Chilean revolution, the Chilean workers paying with the loss of tens of thousands of lives, destruction of their democratic rights, and a steep decline in their already low standard of living.

The development of malignant currents among the Chilean petty bourgeoisie was not at all inevitable. Excellent possibilities existed in that country to win them to the side of the proletariat or at least to neutralize them. In fact, one of the most striking features of the current world political situation, including the situation in Chile when Allende took office, has been the repeated indications of the readiness of class forces closely linked to the proletariat to move in a revolutionary direction.

The upsurge in national liberation struggles, the radicalization of the youth on a scale extending far beyond the proletariat, and the sudden emergence of the women's liberation movement have been especially noteworthy. These promising developments demand close attention. Correctly approached, they can contribute in the most positive way to solving the crisis of proletarian leadership and to forming a revolutionary alliance with broad masses of the petty bourgeoisie.

1. Growing Importance of National Liberation Struggles

The rise of national liberation struggles in all three sectors of the world — the colonial sphere, the imperialist metropolises, and the workers states — is one of the most striking features of the current international political situation. Properly guided, the national liberation movements can be mobilized as a powerful allied force in the proletarian struggle for socialism.

In the imperialist epoch, the national bourgeoisie in

the industrially backward countries betrays its own revolution. Bourgeois democratic tasks, including the achievement of genuine national independence, can be carried out only through the socialist revolution, headed by the proletariat with the support of the urban and rural toiling masses, chiefly the peasants.

The proletarian party must seek to win leadership in the national liberation movements, wresting it from the bourgeois and petty-bourgeois parties. While revolutionary Marxists give no support whatsoever to the alien class program of the bourgeois or petty-bourgeois nationalists, they champion the revolutionary democratic demands of the oppressed masses. The program of Trotskyism stresses the independent class demands of the proletariat and the revolutionary democratic demands of an oppressed people such as a thoroughgoing agrarian reform and national independence. Only this combination enables a revolutionary Marxist party to win leadership in the national liberation struggles and to draw the toiling masses behind the proletariat in a struggle to establish a workers state.

This correct policy on the national question was one of the keys to the victory of the Russian revolution. The main lessons were incorporated in the program of the newly formed Third International, and a promising beginning was made toward the construction of Communist parties in the colonial world. This process was furthered by the worldwide upsurge of national liberation struggles inspired by the example of the Russian revolution.

The growth of Stalinism cut across this development. On the one hand, particularly in the workers movement in the industrially advanced capitalist countries, Stalinism resurrected the concept, prevalent in the pre-1914 Social Democracy, that the national question had no special importance for the proletarian revolution, that it was a peripheral question to be solved in passing by the socialist revolution. On the other hand, in the colonial and semicolonial areas, Stalinism reverted to the old Menshevik "two-stage" theory of revolution, counseling the working class and oppressed masses to look to the bourgeois and petty-bourgeois nationalists as the natural leaders of the "first stage" of the revolution.

Thus the rise of Stalinism helped block the development

of a proletarian leadership of the nationalist movements in the colonial and semicolonial countries. Bourgeois and petty-bourgeois demagogues were able to gain ascendancy in these movements for a prolonged period, portraying themselves without challenge from the Stalinists as the champions of the socialist and nationalist aspirations of the masses.

This reinforced the long detour from the classical pattern of socialist revolution. Many national liberation struggles in the colonial world achieved sufficient strength after World War II to win formal independence from the imperialists; some broke out of the capitalist system as in the cases of China, Cuba, North Vietnam, and North Korea; while others were defeated.

Although formal political independence has been achieved in most of the former colonies of imperialism, national oppression by imperialism continues there in less direct form. The task of winning genuine national liberation still remains to be accomplished.

A good example is the Arab East, where the pressure of imperialism is decisive in maintaining the fragmentation of the Arab people. Arab nationalist consciousness, as expressed in the widespread sentiment for Arab national unification, plays a progressive role in inspiring the Arab masses to struggle against the imperialists, the Zionists, and indigenous reactionary layers opposed to national unification. Of particular importance in advancing the class struggle throughout the Arab world is the Palestinian liberation struggle against the Israeli settler-colonial state.

Under this mass pressure, various bourgeois and petty-bourgeois tendencies have adopted a militant posture as champions of Arab nationalism, Nasserism and Baathism being the chief examples. But these antiproletarian leaderships do not carry out a consistent struggle for their proclaimed nationalist objectives; they continually retreat in face of imperialist pressure. Above all, they fear independent mobilization of the Arab masses, even if it is initially limited to nationalist objectives that they themselves claim to support. Only a revolutionary Marxist party, advancing a rounded class-struggle program, can provide the leadership necessary to carry the struggle through to a socialist revolution, thereby winning the revolutionary nationalist demands raised by the Arab masses.

The national question takes another important form in semicolonial countries where the ruling regimes perpetuate oppression against other nationalities within their own borders, fostering chauvinism by the dominant nationality against them. The Bangladesh national liberation struggle, which exploded in 1971, offers a good example of how struggles against national oppression of this kind can lead to posing the question of workers power.

As the pattern of revolution resumes the classical form of mass urban insurrections, new opportunities open up for constructing revolutionary Marxist parties in the colonial and semicolonial countries. These can be built only by nuclei grounded in the rich Leninist-Trotskyist appreciation of the national question.

In recent years the national question has come into prominence within the imperialist centers themselves. Here the interplay between the democratic struggle against national oppression and the proletarian struggle for the socialist revolution occurs with particular forcefulness because of the high proletarian composition of the oppressed nationalities.

The rise of the Black struggle in the United States in the aftermath of World War II was the first major example of this new development. The colonial revolution inspired the Black masses to struggle for their freedom. The relative quiescence of the working class in the United States reinforced the tendency of the Blacks to rely on themselves and to organize independently.

But this development was not unique. It was followed by the mass Chicano struggles and a growing radicalization of other oppressed nationalities in North America.

In Canada nationalist sentiment within the Québécois working class has been a powerful force helping to fuel the radicalization of labor and affecting all aspects of the class struggle.

In capitalist Europe, the most recent upsurge in the Irish national liberation struggle has been one of the central components of the post-1968 upsurge of the class struggle.

Beginning as a mass movement for democratic rights, demanding an end to the repression required to maintain the division of the country and its subordination to British imperialism, the Irish struggle reached its high point in January-February 1972 when British repression of a large civil-rights demonstration in Derry in the North led to a massive workers mobilization in the formally independent part of the country.

After that, however, the movement went into decline for want of an adequate leadership. The petty-bourgeois nationalists of the Provisional IRA centered on terrorism, while the Official IRA, in turning toward a socialist perspective, slid over to economism, leaving the nationalist-minded masses to the petty-bourgeois nationalists. The far left in Ireland and Britain promoted this degenerative process by idealizing the militarism of the petty-bourgeois nationalists.

The revival of the Irish liberation struggle has given impetus to the development of national democratic movements among the other oppressed nationalities living in Britain and elsewhere in Europe, such as Brittany, for example, where the nationalist groups have traditionally been closely affected by developments in Ireland.

In general, from the Euskara (Basques) in Spain and France to the Koreans in Japan, there has been a growing upsurge of national liberation struggles in the advanced capitalist countries. Even where their numbers are extremely small either relatively or absolutely, as in the case of the Same people (Lapps) in Norway and Sweden, the Native Americans in North America, the Aborigines in Australia, and the Maoris in New Zealand, the struggles of such historically oppressed peoples can have an effect far beyond their size. Growing consciousness of the oppression of such peoples, and support for their struggles against that oppression helps advance the radicalization of the working class as a whole.

The attempts at greater economic coordination among the ruling capitalist classes in Western Europe exacerbate regional inequalities of development, which tend to reflect historical political inequalities. Consequently, the development of nationalist and even separatist movements is likely among the smaller oppressed peoples. Although in many cases these movements may initially reflect the illusions and parochial ambitions of petty local capitalist interests, revolutionary Marxists vigorously support the democratic struggles of such peoples, and challenge the type of economic integration conducted by capitalism.

In cases where minority peoples have some economic advantages but are politically oppressed, as are the Catalans, the generally declining prospects for bourgeois democracy may result in sharp struggles against the bourgeois order. Such struggles may considerably facilitate the task of socialist revolutionaries.

Another aspect of the national question in Western Europe is the struggle of the immigrant workers, who compose an increasingly important proportion of the work force in several countries. Suffering from the worst job conditions and the highest degree of exploitation, and faced by intensifying racist discrimination in daily life, these workers form the potentially most militant and explosive sector of the proletariat.

The rise of national liberation struggles in the imperialist countries has added explosiveness to the social tensions in the urban centers. The class struggle is not reducible to the issues of wages, jobs, and working conditions but takes many forms. It includes the struggle against all types of oppression characteristic of the capitalist era and against all those inherited from previous historical eras, which capitalism perpetuates, extends, and intensifies. The industrial proletariat is the decisive force in the class struggle, but it is not the only component, and it is not sufficient in most countries — it requires allies. Revolutionary Marxists must champion the struggles of all the oppressed, advancing the leadership of the proletariat.

The national question is also of signal importance in the bureaucratized workers states. The struggle against forms of national oppression perpetuated and fostered by the bureaucratic caste is becoming increasingly prominent in Eastern Europe and the Soviet Union. It is emerging as a major component in the political revolution. In the struggle against the menacing rise of bureaucratism in the Soviet Union, which he launched just before his death, Lenin singled out Stalin's reactionary record on the national question as one of the key issues. The

Trotskyist Left Opposition continued the struggle begun by Lenin.

The correctness of this stand was shown in major anti-bureaucratic struggles that broke out following World War II such as the workers upsurge in East Germany in 1953, the Hungarian political revolution in 1956, the Polish upsurge of the same year, and the Czechoslovak explosion in 1968. Each of these upsurges had to confront not only the indigenous Stalinist bureaucracies but above all the Stalinist bureaucracy in Moscow, which attempted to overturn the will of the masses in each of these other countries. Not only does national oppression manifest itself in the Kremlin's military intervention, but also in other ways, such as the subordination of the economic plans of the East European workers states to Soviet needs. Thus, the struggle against national oppression is a key feature of the unfolding political revolution in Eastern Europe.

In the Soviet Union itself national oppression bears down in an even more immediate way. There the bureaucracy has succeeded up to now in maintaining a tight grip on the oppressed nationalities. But the recent growth of antibureaucratic dissidence in the USSR shows that this situation may be changing. Resistance among the Ukrainians, the Baltic peoples, and deported nationalities such as the Crimean Tatars has been on the rise.

The extent of similar movements within China is not known because of the tightness of Peking's censorship.

It is essential for revolutionary Marxist nuclei in the bureaucratized workers states to champion the struggles of oppressed nationalities for liberation from their oppression, including their right to self-determination.

Reactionary political currents have continually attempted to turn the justified anti-Stalinist hostility of the oppressed nationalities against the interests of the workers states and the world revolution. For example, the Zionists have been able to make some gains by basing themselves on Jewish opposition to Stalinist-fostered anti-Semitism. Such dangers make it all the more important for revolutionary Marxists to take the lead in the struggle against national oppression within the Soviet bloc, and to steer it toward a battle for socialist democracy.

As the economy and culture of the workers states advance, the burden of national oppression becomes all the more intolerable; and the interplay between the struggle against national oppression and the antibureaucratic political revolution becomes ever tighter, a development enhanced by the high proletarian composition of the oppressed nationalities in the European workers states.

Of particular importance by virtue of size and strategic position is the struggle of the Ukrainian masses against Great Russian domination. The Fourth International's call for an independent Soviet Ukraine remains in the forefront of the program for political revolution in the USSR.

2. International Radicalization of the Youth

University and high-school youth have in some countries long constituted hotbeds of political ferment, often serving as a sensitive barometer of impending shifts in other layers of the population. Revolutionary movements on all continents have always drawn some of their best cadres from the campus.

In recent decades the school population has greatly expanded as one of the consequences of the need of the capitalist system to provide pools of skilled workers and technicians for industry. Thus the campuses have grown in social weight out of sheer numbers and have been exercising more and more influence in the intellectual and cultural life of most countries. Economic, social, and political crises tend to find sharp and prompt expression among students and their responses easily pass beyond the campus, affecting layers of working-class youth in the factories.

This is, of course, not a one-way process. Working-class struggles can meet with responses of broad scope on the campus. In the final analysis, the political mood of students and teachers is determined by the status of the conflict between wage labor and capital. However, the relationship between the two is not usually direct and immediate. Their development proceeds in an uneven way, each having a logic of its own.

The correctness of these generalizations was borne out to a remarkable degree during the eight years of massive military intervention by U. S. imperialism in Indochina. The antiwar movement took initial form in student protests and teach-ins on key campuses in the United States.

The rebellion on the American campuses, spilling over into the populace as a whole and beginning to affect the ranks of the armed forces, and finally the organized labor movement, was a central reason for the deep tactical division that appeared in the ruling class over the war in Vietnam. This rebellion — coupled with the stubborn resistance of the Vietnamese fighters — compelled Nixon and his business backers to finally withdraw U. S. ground troops from Vietnam.

With this victory, the student movement subsided in the United States. However, it would be a mistake to think that the curtain has now been drawn on American students serving as a source of ferment, and concluding that what they did is now ancient history, never to be repeated. The students that participated in the great demonstrations are now being absorbed into jobs where their experience as active opponents of the war in Vietnam will inevitably find expression in the great working-class struggles that lie ahead.

The younger age levels replacing them on the campus are not much different from them and will respond in a similar way, if not on a higher and more effective level, as further events compel them to assess their perspectives in the light of the realities of capitalist society as a whole.

It should be observed, too, that the Trotskyist movement in the United States has gained from the youth radicalization. The Young Socialist Alliance is now the leading youth organization in the far left in the United States. The Socialist Workers Party likewise expanded in membership and influence as a consequence of the youth radicalization, gaining in particular a new generation of cadres initially recruited to the YSA.

Internationally the most brilliant example of what a student rebellion can lead to was shown in France in May-June 1968. The underlying causes and consequences of that rebellion continue to operate, as has been shown by the big mobilizations among the high-school and university students in France and Belgium against the conscription laws.

Out of the May-June 1968 student rebellion, sizable

forces were won for the Trotskyist movement in France. Before it was banned in 1973, the Ligue Communiste had moved ahead as an increasingly influential force in the far left in Western Europe. In the Fourth International at the time, it ranked as the largest section in the world.

Elsewhere in Europe, the youth radicalization brought fresh forces to the Trotskyist movement in Belgium, Britain, Denmark Germany, Greece, Italy, Spain, Sweden, and Switzerland.

In Argentina the youth radicalization, beginning with mobilizations over "student" issues on the campus, touched off mass mobilizations in the cities. The working-class upsurges in Córdoba, Rosario, Mendoza, and other cities finally compelled the bourgeoisie to retire the military junta and resurrect Perón so as to gain time against the mounting mass movement. In this situation, the Trotskyist movement won several thousand new adherents.

In 1973 the international student movement was again in the headlines. In South Korea demonstrating students gave the Park regime reason for renewed concern over its capacity to retain its grip. In Thailand huge demonstrations, spearheaded by students and backed by workers, shook the government, causing the ruling generals to flee the country. In Greece similar demonstrations, involving a large percentage of workers, caused the officer caste to replace Papadopoulos, hoping by that concession to stave off worse injury to the capitalist government and the system it serves.

The sudden appearance of these three new centers of massive student action served to underline the continuing importance of the youth radicalization on a world scale and its potential in the coming period.

The student protests of the 1960s and 1970s have often combined broad political issues of the class struggle on a national and international scale with issues relating to specific concerns of students. The same expansion of education that increased the social weight of student actions also accentuated the contradictions between the role of the educational system as an institution of capitalist rule and the needs and aspirations of the majority of students.

The mounting economic and social crisis of world capitalism further exacerbates these contradictions. The capitalists in all countries today are compelled to "rational-ize" education: forcing students and their families to pay more of the cost of schooling; tying the content and organization of education even more directly than before to the needs of big business; moving to sharply limit the availability of education other than purely vocational; and instituting measures to restrict students' political free-dom.

These developments lay the basis for increasing sharp conflicts between the students and the capitalist rulers — conflicts of direct concern to the masses of workers, who desire availability of education for their children. Recent instances of such conflicts include the struggles against the Claes-Hurez measures in Belgium; against the Debré law and Fontanet decrees in France; against tuition in-creases and cutbacks in aid to education in Canada, the United States, and other countries; and for increased student grants in Great Britain.

The radicalization of the youth, while opening up extra-ordinary opportunities for the revolutionary-Marxist movement, has also confronted it with difficult challenges. On the political level these stem in the main from the perennial impatience of the youth, which inclines many of them toward ultraleft postures or to simplistic pseudo-solutions to the complex and difficult problem of mobiliz-ing and organizing the working class and its allies in a struggle for power. The same cast of mind opens them to opportunistic turns that can prove just as deadly in divert-ing the movement from a revolutionary course.

Throughout the past decade and a half, this has re-quired consistent battling against New Leftism, Maoism, an-archism, and various other currents of opportunist, ad-venturist, or sectarian bent. Although the rank class-col-laborationism of the Social Democrats and pro-Moscow Stalinists prevented them from making great headway among revolutionary-minded youth during the height of the imperialist aggression in Indochina, they can recover unless a consistent struggle is waged against them. This was demonstrated by the way in which the Stalinists were able to regain positions in the labor movement in various Latin American countries after suffering an eclipse in face of the revolutionary victory in Cuba. The Social Democratic formations in some countries can likewise recuperate by seeming to offer a plausible alternative to socialist-minded young people repelled by Stalinism.

In opposition to these variegated tendencies, the Fourth International, with its program based on the principles of Leninism and Trotskyism, offers another though hard road, requiring the utmost in dedication and self-sacrifice. Only the best in the younger generation of students and workers are capable of following that road to the end, but that end is victory for the cause of worldwide socialism. And follow it they will in the coming period; today in small contingents, tomorrow by the hundreds of thousands and eventually millions.

3. New Rise of Women's Struggles

The international youth radicalization served as a powerful impetus to a new rise of struggles by women. Like the youth radicalization itself, women's liberation also drew inspiration from the colonial struggles and the movements of the oppressed nationalities in the advanced capitalist countries. The character and form of the women's liberation struggles today are rooted in the profound economic and social changes of the post-World War II years, and the deepening contradictions in the status of women and in the patriarchal family system.

In its first stages the women's liberation movement was taken by some to be a North American phenomenon. However, it soon appeared in other countries, and it is continuing to spread in an uneven way. From Australia, New Zealand, and Japan to Britain, France, and Italy, the vangurd of women are speaking a common language, pressing similar issues, and taking similar initiatives in action.

The new rise of women's struggles is a clear index of the depth of the crisis of the bourgeois social order.

Additional proof of this was the fact that in the wake of the women's liberation movement, homosexuals in the United States and other countries began fighting openly for an end to the stigmas attached to their views and practices and for an end to proscription of the right of all humans to freely determine their sexual preferences. In some countries their struggle has advanced significantly in the past few years in gaining public recognition and support of their democratic rights — a telling indication of the far-reaching impact of the deepening political radicalization.

From the beginning, revolutionary Marxists hailed the new upsurge of women's struggles and plunged into the thick of the movement. In doing so, they stood in the tradition of such figures as Marx, Engels, Bebel, Lenin, and Trotsky, who understood the revolutionary significance and importance of women's battles for their liberation.

The Fourth International recognized that the rise of women's struggles was important for the development of the class struggle. This recognition stemmed from the historical materialist analysis of the oppression of women as an indispensable aspect of class society and from an understanding that the patriarchal family is one of the basic institutions of class rule. The struggle of women against their oppression tends to develop in an anticapitalist direction, and is a potentially powerful ally of the working class as a whole in the struggle for socialism. Struggles by women against their oppression provide an avenue to reach and mobilize the most exploited and oppressed layers of the working class. They help to break the stranglehold of reactionary bourgeois ideology, and are part of the battle to educate, politicize and mobilize the entire class around the needs and demands of the most exploited layers.

Many sectarians and ultralefts failed to recognize the importance of the new rise of women's struggles. They either ignored it, abstained from it, or denounced it as "bourgeois feminism." They saw only the fact that it was oftentimes women from petty-bourgeois and even bourgeois backgrounds who first voiced the demands of women. They failed to comprehend the dynamic of the struggle for women's liberation and to recognize that the issues raised were of greatest importance to the most exploited — to those from the working class and oppressed nationalities — and that this would eventually bring these layers to the fore.

They failed to comprehend the interrelationship of women's oppression and class society.

Struggles around issues such as *legalized abortion* — an elementary democratic right — immediately touch on broader oppressive features of class society.

The struggle for women's liberation will, in its normal course of development, encompass and transcend the issues with which it began. It will merge, as a distinct current, into the general struggle of the proletariat for the socialist revolution. The road of this development is quite clear. It will proceed through battling over such issues as the right to *full legal, political and social equality*; *legalized abortion and contraception*; *an end to bourgeois and feudal family law*; *equal educational opportunities*; *job equality* and *equal pay for equal work*; and *government-financed childcare facilities*.

The struggle for women's liberation is interlocked with the proletarian revolution in various ways. Within the organized labor movement it is an important component of the general battle to transform the unions into instruments of revolutionary struggle by convincing the most conscious workers to take up and fight for the needs and demands of the most oppressed and exploited layers of the class. Directly involved in this is the role of the trade unions in safeguarding and advancing the standard of living of the workers as a whole. Revolutionists should take the lead in pressing the trade unions to fight for the demands raised by women in industry and outside.

A similarly important interrelationship between the women's liberation movement and the proletarian revolution is offered by the struggle for national liberation. Women oppressed because of their nationality as well as their sex and status as workers may join the struggle for national liberation. But this struggle itself moves toward socialism in search of final solutions to the problems that have created it. Consequently women involved in national liberation movements are drawn in the direction of revolutionary socialism. They see socialism as a triple revolution — against wage slavery, against sexism, against national oppression.

Forms of struggle must be developed capable of mobilizing masses of women, awakening their creative capacities and initiatives, bringing them together, destroying their domestic isolation, increasing their confidence in their own abilities, their own intelligence, independence, and strength.

Through their own battles women will have to learn who are their class allies and who are their enemies. They will come to understand the interrelationship between their oppression as a sex and class exploitation, and the need for proletarian methods of struggle which reject all forms of class collaboration.

Participating in these battles, revolutionary Marxists will be able to demonstrate in action that our perspectives, program and fighting capacities are capable of providing the kind of leadership necessary.

The default of the Stalinists and Social Democrats, and the sectarian foolishness of the ultralefts, make the new rise of women's struggles of special importance to the Fourth International as an arena where new cadres can be won and where our limited forces can gain valuable experience that can be applied in other areas of the class struggle.

As Trotsky said in 1938: "The decay of capitalism . . . deals its heaviest blows to the woman as a wage-earner and as a housewife. The sections of the Fourth International should seek bases of support among the most exploited layers of the working class, consequently among the women workers. Here they will find inexhaustible stores of devotion, selflessness and readiness to sacrifice."

IV. Mobilization of the Counterrevolution and the Struggle Against It

1. Blockade of Cuba and the "Caribbean Confrontation"

U. S. imperialism had every reason to stand in fear of the Cuban revolution and its repercussions. As a consequence, the containment and crushing of the Cuban revolution became of primary concern to the State Department, the Central Intelligence Agency, and the Pentagon. Under Eisenhower, the White House placed an economic blockade on the island, mounted a diplomatic offensive, and prepared an invasion that was brought to a head by Kennedy in the Bay of Pigs military assault.

The Cubans, supported by an energetic solidarity movement inside the United States itself, succeeded in defeating the armed imperialist intervention for the time being.

It was clear, however, that the Cuban people on their small island could not withstand a better prepared invasion by the most powerful military establishment the world has yet seen. To bolster their defenses they sought nuclear-tipped rocket installations from the Soviet Union, which, as Castro stated, was their right as a sovereign power.

This resulted in the famous Caribbean confrontation between Kennedy and Khrushchev in which the American president threatened to plunge the world into a nuclear holocaust if Khrushchev did not withdraw the rockets. Khrushchev backed down in face of Kennedy's threat.

Out of the confrontation came the "Caribbean détente" between Moscow and Washington, the terms of which remain secret to this day. It is evident, however, that they included an agreement whereby the White House promised not to mount another invasion of Cuba, while the Kremlin promised to limit the types of weapons it would release to Havana. The détente included mutual tolerance of Washington's continuance of the economic blockade and Moscow's compensating for this by sending material aid in substantial amounts.

Castro and Guevara, to their credit, understood the necessity of extending the Cuban revolution if it was to survive in the long run. In this respect they took an internationalist stand, fostering and supporting revolutionary struggles elsewhere in the world, above all in Latin America. The organization of OLAS in 1967 and Guevara's project of a guerrilla front in Bolivia stemmed directly from this internationalist view.

Limitations in the education and outlook of the Cuban leaders blocked success in their efforts to extend the Cuban revolution. They were not Leninists. They did not set out to organize a solid political base by fostering the organization of mass revolutionary parties standing on the program of revolutionary Marxism. Immediately following the revolutionary victory in Havana, the situation was extraordinarily favorable for this inasmuch as millions of Latin Americans were lifted to their feet by what had been accomplished in toppling Batista and moving forward to the establishment of a planned economy in the Caribbean.

The Cuban leaders not only missed their timing in this but committed a series of ultraleft errors. Still worse, they decried "theory" as compared to "practice," and reduced practice to guerrillaism on a continental scale. The guerrilla strategy proved to be sterile, and since the defeat of Guevara's effort in Bolivia, the Cubans have virtually abandoned it.

The guerrillaism of the Cubans was quite logically coupled with depreciation of the validity and importance of revolutionary political principles. One of the gravest manifestations of this shortcoming came in their relations with the Kremlin. In return for material aid — without which, of course, the Cuban revolution could not have survived for long — the Cuban leaders granted undue political concessions to the Soviet ruling caste, helping to a certain degree to provide the Russian bureaucrats with a left cover.

A prime example was the apologies offered by Castro for the Soviet military invasion that crushed the budding political revolution in Czechoslovakia in 1968 that might have replaced the Stalinist regime there with proletarian democracy.

In a parallel way, Castro has offered political support to bourgeois regimes in Latin America that have maintained diplomatic relations with Cuba. Conspicuous examples were Goulart in Brazil, Velasco Alvarado in Peru, and Allende in Chile. It is, of course, correct for the Cuban government to try to establish and to keep up diplomatic relations with all other governments, no matter what economic, social, and political system they represent. What is impermissible from the revolutionary-Marxist point of view is to express political solidarity with them, since this signifies placing confidence in the bourgeoisie and their policies, an act that disorients and diverts the workers movement in those countries from the revolutionary road. The catastrophe in Chile stands out as a grim example of what can result under such regimes, however loudly they proclaim that their aim is the achievement of socialism.

The mistakes made by the Cuban leaders helped open the way for the Stalinists to stage a comeback in Latin America. Even in Venezuela, where they had come under fierce denunciations from Castro in 1967 because of their treachery, they were able to reestablish themselves at the expense of the Guevarists.

Before the establishment of the military dictatorships in Uruguay and Chile, the Stalinists gained a free hand to engage in popular frontism behind Seregni and Allende to the detriment of the class struggle and particularly the defense of the Cuban revolution.

Castro's political softness toward the Kremlin has also had its domestic reflection. From 1961 to 1968, great concern was felt over the bureaucratic tendency forming around Aníbal Escalante, a Stalinist leader of the old class-collaborationist Cuban Communist party, and stern measures were taken to push this tendency back. Castro now appears to be following a policy of "peaceful co-existence" with Cuban bureaucratism. One notable consequence has been strictures on free thought and artistic expression (the Héberto Padilla affair for instance). This has damaged the prestige of the Cuban government, bringing severe criticism from long-standing supporters of the Cuban revolution.

The failure of the Castro team to advance toward the establishment in Cuba of proletarian forms of democracy such as the soviets of the early years of the Russian revolution, in which various organized political tendencies and factions that supported the revolution were able to openly criticize defects and mobilize rank-and-file support in behalf of remedial measures, constitutes one of the gravest weaknesses in the Cuban governmental system. It nourishes subterranean currents, particularly those of a rightist bureaucratic character. These degenerative developments can break into the open with stunning abruptness, perhaps catching even a Fidel Castro by surprise. To forestall such an eventuality and to ensure full mobilization of the masses in defense of the revolution, institutions of workers democracy should be formed in Cuba along the lines of those that functioned in the Soviet Union in the early days under Lenin.

The establishment in December 1973 of rankings in the armed forces equivalent to those in the capitalist countries and the bureaucratized workers states constituted another step on the road away from proletarian democracy. It marked the open appearance of a privileged officer caste, revealing how far bureaucratization has proceeded in the armed forces.

Consequently, it must be acknowledged that the Cuban revolution has not realized its initial potentialities in helping to resolve the crisis of proletarian leadership internationally. In serious respects the Cuban leaders have fallen back, while dangerous bureaucratic tendencies continue to gather headway.

Under the following slogans, the Fourth International remains, as it has been from the beginning, the most intransigent defender of the Cuban revolution:

For unconditional defense of the Cuban revolution against imperialist attack.

For an end to Washington's blockade of Cuba. Let the United States give up its naval base in Guantánamo.

For diplomatic recognition of the Cuban government by all other governments.

For free trade with Cuba and the granting of credits and material aid.

For extension of the Cuban victory throughout Latin America.

2. The U. S. Imperialist Intervention in Vietnam

The eight years from February 1965, when Johnson ordered the first major military assault on North Vietnam, to January 1973, when a cease-fire was signed in Paris, marked a great turning point in postwar history.

At the outset of 1965 imperialist America appeared to have reached a pinnacle in dominance, a consequence of its victory in World War II. Its nuclear stockpile was sufficient to obliterate all the higher forms of life on the planet many times over. In the imperialist sector, it outweighed by far any combination of its capitalist rivals. It was prosperous enough to give plausibility to the propaganda about an "affluent society" and Johnson's demagogy about the feasibility of eliminating poverty in the United States. To blot out the rebellious tendencies in the colonial world and to further constrict "communism" seemed a relatively easy matter, involving only small "brushfire" conflicts like the Bay of Pigs operation in Cuba. This was how things appeared when Johnson decided to intervene in the civil war in Vietnam in a vigorous way.

What was revealed by the conflict? The American colossus proved to have feet of clay. The colonial revolution was stronger than the White House strategists had calculated. The industrially backward, agrarian Democratic Republic of Vietnam survived the most murderous and destructive assault in history on such a small country. The imperialist goliath was weakened sufficiently to encourage other small countries to offer stiffer resistance. In the United States, the vaunted prosperity was seriously undermined, and the almighty dollar declined dramatically.

Wall Street's imperialist rivals gained better bargaining positions.

In Vietnam itself Washington had to accept an outcome much below what had been confidently anticipated in the beginning. Nixon could count himself fortunate that he had rescue teams in Moscow and Peking able to save him from ending up with a first-rate disaster in Vietnam.

The full costs of this "brush-fire" war are not yet reliably known. Saigon has admitted that its own casualties included at least 320,000 troops, and has claimed a higher figure for North Vietnam. The civilian casualties were much greater. Refugees number in the millions.

The cost to Vietnam is directly visible in the landscape, much of which now resembles that of the moon because of the cratering. The Pentagon's carpet-bombing and use of herbicides to destroy crops and forests on a vast scale has led to irreversible destruction of the soil in some areas and will have deleterious effects in others for generations to come.

In conjunction with the close of the long postwar boom cycle, the war placed fresh strains on the U.S. economy, exacerbating inflationary trends. The cost to the U.S. Treasury has been estimated conservatively at $600 billion.

Domestic social tensions were greatly heightened as evidenced by the deepening radicalization. On the campuses, students staged militant demonstrations, often taking the offensive in advancing their own interests as students against the school administration and their governmental backers. Opposition was especially sharp to conscription into the armed forces and to military recruiting efforts on the campus. The movement for Black liberation built up to new heights, scorning all appeals to give up the struggle temporarily in behalf of the war. The workers refused to believe in the war propaganda, and rejected making any economic sacrifices to help the intervention in Vietnam. In face of the appeals to their patriotism, they continued to defend their standard of living through union bargaining and strike struggles. The armed forces were seriously affected by the widespread mood of resistance to authority.

The political consequences were marked by the forced retirement of Johnson from public life and the development of a climate in which the impeachment of "the president" became a popular demand.

The decision to intervene in Vietnam in a massive way accorded with the overall plans for world conquest held by U.S. imperialism since the end of World War II. The White House took the plunge into a war on the Asian mainland because it thought the rift between Peking and Moscow could be made to pay off militarily through a bold stroke.

The geopoliticians of the U.S. military establishment likewise thought that by bringing the mailed fist down with sufficient brutality and ruthlessness they could strike terror throughout the colonial world, converting Vietnam into a fearful object lesson to other peoples dreaming of winning their freedom. The Pentagon's slogan could have been formulated as "No more Cubas!"

The calculations of the Pentagon proved to be partially correct. Moscow and Peking showed themselves incapable of closing ranks sufficiently to put up a united front against the common imperialist foe whose thrusts were in the final analysis aimed at them. They refrained from sponsoring mass protest demonstrations on an international scale. Although it was well within their means, they were unwilling to provide sufficient weaponry and supplies to the Democratic Republic of Vietnam and the National Liberation Front to assure a military victory over the imperialist invader. They even stood aside in face of Nixon's bombing of Hanoi and his decision to mine all the harbors of North Vietnam so as to block delivery of Soviet and Chinese supplies of food and materiel.

Moreover, the North Vietnamese leaders remained true to their training in the school of Stalinism. While they offered a stubborn battle on the military level, they did not match it with a Leninist political course. Instead of advancing a program for socialism in South Vietnam, which would have aroused the masses there as nothing else could, they called for a bourgeois coalition government. They did not even raise independent demands for the working class. This stance was reflected in their attitude toward U.S. imperialism. They did not engage in socialist propaganda in the exemplary Bolshevik way to hasten disintegration of the invading armies and turn

discontented U. S. troops into emissaries of socialism in
America itself. They relied strictly on slogans related to
the right of national self-determination. It was completely
correct to stand on this right and to defend it to the death;
but a revolutionary-socialist program would have added
a qualitatively superior political force to the defense of
the Vietnamese revolution. Hanoi's course was patterned
on Stalin's attitude during the "patriotic war" against German imperialism but without emulating Stalin in his ex-
cesses.

All this entered into the calculations of the White House.
What was overlooked or discounted was the possibility
of effective popular resistance under these unfavorable
circumstances. The miscalculation was a grave one—
it involved two key areas, Vietnam and the United States.

In Vietnam the masses rallied in a way comparable
to that of the Russian people in defending their revolution
in 1918-20 against the Allied imperialist intervention and
in 1941-45 against the German imperialist invasion.
Through their prolonged heroic resistance, they converted
Vietnam from the easily seized Asian beachhead the Pentagon dreamed of into a quagmire into which the American
military machine sank deeper and deeper.

On the other side of the Pacific in the United States the
opposition to the war was immediate and widespread,
taking overt form on the campuses from the beginning.
This popular resistance was something new in imperialist
America.

In World War I, the country was at first swept with patriotic hysteria. In World War II, the attitude was much
more subdued, the general feeling being that there was
no escaping going into battle against Hitler, Mussolini,
and the Mikado. In the Korean conflict, opposition appeared within months, and it grew to such an extent as
to doom the Democratic bid for the White House in 1952.
But it did not express itself in large-scale mass demonstrations.

In the intervention in Vietnam, however, the opposition
was able to stage huge rallies and marches in cities from
coast to coast and to repeatedly converge on Washington
and other key centers in a way that began to accustom the
country to voicing protests in an organized way in the

streets, thus encouraging extraparliamentary political action in the main citadel of world capitalism.

A feature of the highest significance was the initiative taken by the organizers of these demonstrations to reach out internationally and to appeal for protests in a coordinated way. Thus, throughout this entire period the world saw something absolutely new — groups in cities on all continents staging simultaneous demonstrations, often involving huge assemblages. For instance, in coordination with protests in the United States, cities like London, Paris, Melbourne, and Tokyo witnessed turnouts of as high as 100,000 persons.

The world saw something else that was new. The biggest demonstrations occurred inside the United States itself while the country was involved in a war planned, precipitated, and supported by the two capitalist parties that hold an absolute monopoly on the entire American governmental system from top to bottom, including Congress.

Some of the antiwar demonstrations in cities like New York, San Francisco, and Washington were of a size never before seen, reaching up to one million persons on a single day.

Confidence in the governmental institutions of American capitalist society suffered a good deal of erosion. In the form of a growing "credibility gap," dissatisfaction with both the Republicans and Democrats has continued to spread in popular consciousness.

Special attention should be paid to the advanced nature of the main slogans that surged to the fore in the American antiwar movement. The central one was *"For self-determination of the Vietnamese people."* This took the form — and within the imperialist country mounting the aggression! — of the demand *"Withdraw U. S. troops now!"* These slogans, echoed by millions of Americans, powerfully aided the struggling Vietnamese in their battle for freedom, as the Vietnamese leaders themselves acknowledged.

The Fourth International can justly be proud of the fact that the Trotskyist movement played a key role within the imperialist aggressor country itself in bringing these slogans to the fore and in assuring that the antiwar movement took the form of a gigantic mobilization that caught public attention in many other countries, thereby helping antiwar militants internationally to engage in meaningful actions aimed at facilitating the victory of the NLF.

As the Vietnam war unfolded, the antiwar movement also began to have a noticeable effect on the morale of the U. S. troops. The broadening domestic disaffection over Johnson and Nixon's prolongation of the war bolstered oppositionist moods among the GIs, where they took forms that increasingly alarmed the Pentagon. The American forces in Southeast Asia threatened to come apart as they had at the end of World War II. This phenomenon was all the more remarkable in view of the failure of the North Vietnamese to bombard the GIs with leaflets, pamphlets, and radio messages explaining socialism and seeking to win them over to it. The program of socialism was brought to the GIs through the efforts of the Trotskyists, who distributed literature to them in the United States, Japan, Western Europe, etc., in areas where they were stationed or in transit.

As it mounted, the American antiwar movement also succeeded in involving more and more workers. Towards the end, sectors of organized labor that became disturbed over the continued support to the war offered by the top AFL-CIO officialdom began to take action, a development that chilled ruling circles, sharpening the divisions among them over what tactic to follow.

When Nixon announced on April 30, 1970, that he had ordered an invasion of Cambodia, the American students gave his surprise move a surprise reply — the biggest spontaneous explosion of campus protest seen in history. It was during this wave that the National Guard fired on protesting students at Kent University, and the police slayed Black students at Jackson, Mississippi, murderous acts that intensified the spontaneous reaction. Millions of students went on strike. In many areas students took over their campuses, turning them into "antiwar universities," that is, organizing centers to expand the protests throughout the country.

To meet this deepening protest movement, Nixon resorted among other things to police-state methods, sending provocateurs into the antiwar movement, the Black liberation movement, and radical groupings, engaging in tapping of telephones, intimidation, harassment, police attacks, shootings of demonstrators, and frame-up trials. As happened during the McCarthyite period, in which Nixon shaped his political career, these antidemocratic methods were eventually turned against the liberal wing of the Democratic party, becoming epitomized in the burglaries that made "Watergate" a household word around the globe.

The enduring consequences inside the United States of the Vietnam war constitute a new element in world politics. From now on, direct involvement of U.S. troops on a sizable scale anywhere outside of the country is certain to meet with militant opposition domestically, with the likelihood of that opposition broadening rapidly into a colossal force.

Even if the U.S. ruling class were to refrain from engaging in new military adventures for the foreseeable future — which is unlikely — the change in political climate points toward a deepening radicalization of the working class and its allies in the period ahead, no matter how the rate of this process may be affected by conjunctural dips. The economic costs of the war, which are being passed on to the workers, help assure continuation of this trend.

3. Violent Repression and Class Collaborationism

With their various forms of fascism between the first and second world wars, Mussolini, Pilsudski, Hitler, and Franco signaled the new barbarism implicit in the evolution of capitalism. The trend has not been reversed since Hitler's gas ovens. The murder of as many as one million suspected "Communists" by the genocidal Suharto regime in Indonesia in 1965 proved that. The reigns of terror that have existed for a decade in Brazil and still longer in Iran, Paraguay, and South Africa speak in the same sense. In 1973 Chile's "nonpolitical" generals added their bit to the evidence by cold-bloodedly deciding on "a new Jakarta." The readiness of the capitalist class to resort to naked violence and ferocious terror if its rule is seriously challenged has clearly become more and more marked in the period of the death agony of the capitalist system.

The regimes that engage in mass murder to liquidate the labor movement and smother the revolutionary aspirations of the workers and their allies do not appear suddenly out of the nether world. They are preceded by phases in the class struggle that provide opportunities for revolutionary victories. In these phases, militant currents can grow swiftly, opening the way for the rise of a Leninist-type party of mass proportions.

In view of this potentiality, the capitalist rulers are prepared in advance to resort to the most extreme violence. However, they are never certain of the outcome of such measures, and prefer other means to keep the masses in check — and also to help provide more favorable conditions for the counterrevolution. Thus they utilize political stratagems of the most deceptive nature to divert the masses from taking the road of revolution.

In the imperialist countries, the capitalist rulers bend to the pressure. In meeting the May-June 1968 situation in France, de Gaulle granted economic concessions. In the United States during the industrial strife of the thirties, Roosevelt granted liberal-democratic concessions, recognizing in particular labor's right to organize.

In the colonial and semicolonial world, where the resources available to the bourgeoisie are much more limited, any far-reaching concessions or extended periods of bourgeois democracy are, of course, excluded. Nevertheless, the bourgeoisie — or at least its shrewdest layers — seek to bend with the pressure there, too. Examples of this abound, a striking instance being the concessions granted in Argentina under the first regime of General Juan D. Perón.

The flexibility of some leaders of the national bourgeoisie is noteworthy. They are capable not only of granting concessions to the masses but of combining these with actions against the imperialists. Chiang Kai-shek fought for a number of years against the Japanese imperialist invasion of China. Mossadegh nationalized the British-owned oil industry in Iran. Sukarno opposed Dutch and American imperialism. Nasser took over the Suez

Canal and held it in face of a military invasion mounted by British and French imperialism abetted by Israel.

In Latin America many examples can be cited of anti-imperialist actions taken by the "statesmen" of the national bourgeoisie. General Lázaro Cárdenas, the president of Mexico, expropriated the oil holdings of the Americans and British. General Perón resisted both British and American imperialism in Argentina. General Juan Velasco Alvarado is currently practicing "military reformism" in Peru at the expense of some of the companies on the New York stock exchange. Salvador Allende nationalized various American imperialist holdings.

Political representatives of the national bourgeoisie are capable of taking on a most deceptive revolutionary coloration, posing as strongly pro-Moscow or pro-Peking or both, and making themselves out to be protagonists of "socialist" economic planning. Chiang Kai-Shek — with Stalin's aid — wrapped himself in the Soviet flag before the 1925-27 Chinese revolution. Sukarno sought and obtained the endorsement of Mao Tsetung. Nasser leaned heavily on Moscow in shaping his image of "socialist" innovation in Egypt. Nkrumah in Ghana and Ne Win in Burma followed similar courses. In his final years, Cárdenas posed as an admirer of Fidel Castro and the Cuban revolution.

The anti-imperialist measures taken by the national bourgeoisie are always incomplete and transitory. Cases of involvement of the workers, as in Mexico under Cárdenas or in Argentina under Perón, are ephemeral. The commitment of the national bourgeoisie to capitalism makes it impossible for them to gain real national independence from imperialism. They have no choice in the final analysis but to bow to the imperious pressures of the world market.

The anti-imperialist actions undertaken by national bourgeois regimes warrant the support of revolutionary Marxists. This support should take the form wherever possible of mass demonstrations, the bigger the better. This is the proletarian form of action par excellence. Such mobilizations of the workers and their allies should be organized in support of specific anti-imperialist *measures* — and *not* in support of the bourgeois figures who feel compelled to take them.

In no case can revolutionary Marxists give *political support* to regimes of the national bourgeoisie, no matter how progressive they may appear to be. Innumerable experiences prove that the opposition of the national bourgeoisie to imperialism is highly unstable. The national bourgeoisies will not conduct a consistent struggle against imperialism. Trotsky long ago explained the reasons. First of all, if the working class and peasantry are mobilized, they tend, in following their own class interests, to break through the framework of capitalism. This tendency has become an increasingly paramount feature of the political scene. Secondly, the main class interests of the national bourgeoisie are the same as those of the imperialists, and they serve as their agents. Often their major objective in seizing foreign holdings is to improve their bargaining position as agencies of imperialism.

In fact, by sowing illusions among the masses, these same regimes disarm the workers and their allies, facilitating the succeeding phase of terror directed against them. In this way, too, the "progressive" sector of the national bourgeoisie plays a counterrevolutionary role despite the actions it may take against imperialism.

In both the colonial and imperialist countries, the petty-bourgeois bureaucracies of the trade unions and the Social Democratic and Stalinist parties play an especially treacherous role in paving the way for the coups of the military caste or fascist formations. They accomplish this through the politics of *class collaborationism*.

In the United States the trade-union bureaucracy carries on class collaborationism without disguise or apologies. Openly espousing the possibility of winning lasting reforms under capitalism, it participates in upholding the capitalist two-party system as a loyal faction in either the Republican or Democratic parties, principally the latter.

In Great Britain the trade-union bureaucracy operates through the Labour party, which has formally been committed to socialist objectives in the past, but which has practiced the rankest class collaborationism, actually conducting the affairs of state for the bourgeoisie in times of stress. So long as they themselves are too weak to offer an effective opposition in the electoral arena, revolutionary Marxists call for casting a vote for Labour party candidates. Such a vote is not cast for the *platform* of the reformist leadership of the Labour party.

The creation of the Labour party was a tremendous positive achievement of the working class. However, the Labour party has long played a negative role, harnessing the working class to reformism and class-collaborationism. Against capitalist reaction, revolutionary Marxists stand on the side of the Labour party and seek to increase its weight as a massive political force. But the primary purpose of calling for a vote for reformist candidates of the Labour party is to help speed the process of exposing them as watchdogs of the bourgeoisie. Another objective is to bolster the tendency of the working-class ranks of the Labour party to move in a militant, class-struggle direction in opposition to the party's bureaucratic leadership.

While calling for a Labour vote under these conditions, revolutionary Marxists attack the reformist leaders and advance an alternative program of transitional proposals designed to give impetus to the struggle for a workers government.

Revolutionary Marxists follow the same line with respect to other Social Democratic parties around the world that have a mass working-class base, ranging from Canada, Australia, and Japan to Belgium, France, and Germany.

Revolutionary Marxists take a comparable stand toward the Communist parties in the capitalist world that have a mass working-class base.

A *united front* of two or more mass reformist labor parties is a possibility in some countries. A development of this kind would represent a step forward warranting critical support from revolutionists on the basis of the line of class opposition drawn between the labor and bourgeois parties. In cases of this kind, the Trotskyist movement would press for implementation of the united front in the extraparliamentary arena with the objective of establishing a workers and peasants government.

Unlike a united front that draws a line of opposition to the bourgeoisie, *"people's frontism,"* which has constituted the axis of Stalinist politics in the capitalist world since 1935, represents a variety of class collaborationism. Like the reformist labor parties, a people's front appeals to the illusions of the working class in the bourgeois electoral system and bourgeois coalition governments. It seeks to reinforce these illusions in order to divert the workers from taking the road to revolution. It consciously opposes extraparliamentary action, and when this kind of action cannot be avoided, it seeks to limit it and divert it into "safe" channels. Moreover, in a people's front, the Stalinists utilize the prestige of the Soviet Union, or other workers states, in this dirty game.

The distinguishing feature of a people's front is the open inclusion of bourgeois parties in the electoral front as a sector either in charge of determining policies or in whose interests policies are deliberately shaped. If, for the moment, substantial bourgeois parties are not prepared to participate in a people's front, the Stalinists readily accept surrogates, no matter how shadowy they may be. To call for a vote for a people's front therefore signifies supporting an *electoral platform to advance class collaborationism.* A question of principle is involved. To vote for such a platform is not a tactical question like giving critical support to a labor party (even one participating in a people's front) in order to bring it into office so as to expose in the most convincing way possible the treacherous nature of its leadership before its mass base.

The Union of the Left (Union de la Gauche) in France is a current example of a people's front. While it is not identical to the "classical" people's front of the mid-thirties in France, it bears a strong family resemblance.

In the thirties, the people's front set up by the Stalinists in many countries claimed to have the objective of "stopping fascism." Under the changed circumstances of the seventies, the Stalinists put "socialism" to the fore. The seeming shift was designed to meet conjunctural needs and does not signify an alteration in the basic content of the people's front, which remains class collaborationism.

The People's Unity (Unidad Popular) that backed Salvador Allende in Chile offered an instructive example of the continuity in the Stalinist line. Like the Union of the Left in France, this people's front proclaimed "socialism" as its ultimate goal. In its final days, however, the propaganda stress shifted to "stopping fascism" in the style of the various people's fronts of the mid-thirties.

These two current cases, along with the Broad Front (Frente Amplio) in Uruguay, show that people's frontism is still thriving despite its counterrevolutionary consequences in the thirties in France, Spain, Cuba, and many other countries, both imperialist and colonial, and in the sixties in countries like Brazil, Ceylon, and Indonesia.

It should be noted that in advancing and practicing people's frontism, Moscow and Peking offer little to choose between. Both Mao and Brezhnev are apt disciples of Stalin, the arch exponent of this variety of Menshevism and class collaborationism.

Mao bore direct responsibility for the policies of the Indonesian Communist party under Aidit that led to the victory of Suharto, a catastrophe comparable to the outcome of Stalin's policies in Germany in 1933. During the subsequent mass slaughter there were reports of guerrilla activities in various parts of Indonesia. The reports were either exaggerated by Peking, were faked by Suharto to cover continuing executions of batches of "Communists," or were desperate rearguard actions that ended in demoralization and prostration. This is clear eight years later.

In Chile from 1970 to 1973, the Moscow-oriented Communist party headed by Corvalán followed a people's front policy that went so far as to hail the inclusion of bourgeois generals in the coalition government. The "army-party," as it has been called by some, utilized its cabinet posts to undermine the "socialist" president and to prepare in detail the military coup that finished the new experiment in people's frontism. The blow constituted a major setback for the entire Latin American revolution.

Two lessons stand out with glaring clarity in the Chilean debacle — the need for a revolutionary party and the need to puncture the delusion that a "peaceful road to socialism" can be found through class collaborationism and the election of a coalition government.

In all its modern variations, class collaborationism calls for the same opposition from revolutionary Marxists as previous varieties going back to the Kerenskyism of 1917 in Russia, which Trotsky called the "people's front" of that time, and still further back to the Millerandism that was energetically battled by the left wing of the Social Democracy in the years before 1914.

The political essence of reformism and people's front-ism, whatever the variants, consists — let it be repeated — of *class collaborationism*. That is what revolutionary Marxists focus on in combating it.

The class-struggle alternative offered by revolutionary Marxists has various forms, ranging from opposition in the electoral arena to extraparliamentary action that eventually reaches the level of armed struggle for power. Its essence, however, consists of *independent working-class political action,* which reaches its highest forms under the leadership provided by a Leninist-type party.

Independent political action constitutes the means whereby the working class will eventually overcome the counter-revolutionary politics practiced by the capitalist rulers, whether ultrareactionary, liberal, or deceptively anti-imperialist. Independent political action also constitutes the means whereby the working class will overcome the class-collaborationist politics practiced by the trade-union, Social Democratic, and Stalinist bureaucracies.

4. "Peaceful Coexistence" and the Detente

In Vietnam, the Pentagon experienced the difficulty of smashing a revolution solely by military means even if used on a scale verging on the employment of nuclear weapons. The test was all the more impressive because the Pentagon had the supplementary advantages offered by the Sino-Soviet rift and the policy followed by both Moscow and Peking of limiting material aid to Hanoi and the National Liberation Front.

The deleterious consequences to the world standing of the United States resulting from the Pentagon's inability to achieve the main goal it had set in Vietnam, namely, to blot out the liberation struggle, led U. S. imperialism to make a turn in policy toward the Soviet and Chinese ruling castes. Nixon and Kissinger engaged in the "summitry" that brought Moscow and Peking into a common front with Washington against the advance of the world revolution. The common front, depicted as "peaceful coexistence" by Moscow and Peking, called for unity in action, a good deal of it in secret, while leaving leeway for mutual criticism in public.

This was the real meaning of Moscow and Peking's participation, under Nixon's sponsorship, in the behind-the-scenes negotiations that led to the "cease-fire" signed in January 1973.

The White House wanted the cooperation of Moscow and Peking in the imperialist effort to contain the Vietnamese revolution. The immediate objective was to help the Pentagon withdraw U. S. ground troops "with honor," and to use Soviet and Chinese influence for the time being as a substitute for U. S. troops and bombers.

For this cooperation, Nixon was willing to pay a price. Moscow received some concessions in the form of a lowering of trade barriers and removal of the ban on shipment of most "strategic goods." Peking received similar concessions plus membership in the United Nations, the opening of diplomatic relations, and ending of the game of picturing Chiang Kai-shek's regime as the legitimate government of China.

America's imperialist rulers had additional concerns in mind. Inside the imperialist bloc itself, the mood of the masses, as evidenced by the growth and actions of the antiwar movement in North America and the rise in workers struggles in Western Europe and elsewhere, endangered further militaristic advances abroad, calling in fact for a relaxation of tensions if not the granting of concessions to bring the situation under better control.

Furthermore, the growth of interimperialist rivalries required attention. The capitalist countries that had been saved from the threat of revolution at the end of World War II by such measures as the Marshall Plan and the occupation of Japan had now become annoying competitors. The cost of the aggression in Indochina was weakening the American economy, particularly in the form of intensified inflation. The decline of the dollar was an ominous sign of what was happening to the relative standing of the United States. Even the governments of small countries like Peru, highly dependent on Wall Street, were daring to nationalize holdings of American corporations.

A detente with Moscow and Peking, permitting a withdrawal from Vietnam under the best possible circumstances, including retention of the Saigon beachhead, would facilitate opening a counteroffensive at home against the labor movement, which was pressing more and more heavily for wage increases to make up for the losses caused by inflation. A detente would likewise facilitate putting America's imperialist rivals back in their places. It would, for instance, help cut into trade with the Soviet bloc which had virtually been monopolized by the West European countries and Japan.

Washington's detente with Moscow and Peking could hardly be opposed by Tokyo, Bonn, London, or Paris, although it signified gains for American capitalism at their expense. These powers stand today in the position of Great Britain in the twenties when the former mistress of the seas backed down from a confrontation that could have led to war with the United States. Britain's rulers prudently decided at that time that they had no realistic choice but to accept a role subordinate to that of the new colossus in the affairs of international capitalism. Today, Japan and the West European powers have no choice but to bow even more humbly before the Nixons, Kissingers, and Connallys. This was shown rather dramatically by the meekness in tone in their complaints at being excluded from the secret negotiations over the Middle East war in October 1973 and by the way they dropped to their knees when the American oil barons suddenly tightened the valves on their oil supplies. The fact is that even a combination of all the West European powers, plus Japan, could not stand up effectively as capitalist states against American imperialism with its fleets of submarines, intercontinental rockets, space satellites, and stockpiles of nuclear weapons, nerve gases, and bacteria.

In addition, the strategists of American imperialism saw a priceless opportunity to intervene in the Sino-Soviet rift. By adroit diplomacy, Washington could gain the advantageous position of acting as "moderator" between Peking and Moscow—for the sake of "world peace," of course—judiciously playing one against the other in the process, while undermining both of them.

Thus in a complete reversal of Truman's postwar stance of dangling the atom bomb over the Kremlin, the White House has now assumed the posture of being the best friend of the bureaucrats in Moscow—and Peking. More amazing still, the turn was carried out by Nixon, one of the McCarthyite specialists in witch-hunting the State Department to root out the hidden "Commies" who caused the U. S. to "lose China."

Startling as the reversal may appear to be, it hardly represents something new. Truman practiced "peaceful co-existence" with Tito. Before that Roosevelt gave a masterful performance with Stalin.

These zigzags in Washington's foreign policy do not represent an oscillation between a completely counterrevolutionary line and a "soft on communism" line. Such an interpretation is a pretext used by the Stalinists to justify their policy of participating in the wheeling and dealing of capitalist politics where they try to bolster the liberals and put pressure on them to resist the hard line of the anti-Communist "hawks."

Moscow and Peking see the detente as the consummation of the class-collaborationist policy each has pursued for decades as the bureaucratic alternative to the revolutionary internationalism practiced by Lenin and Trotsky before the degeneration of the first workers state. Stalin's policy in this respect is well known. Mao's course before the detente was more veiled because of the persistent rejection of his overtures by U. S. imperialism. The limited aid given by Mao to guerrilla groupings in various parts of the world, his efforts to set up "pro-Chinese" groupings, and his revolutionary-sounding verbal denunciations of American imperialism constituted pressure for an understanding that was outlined in public as long ago as the Bandung Conference in 1955.

Moscow and Peking's chief motivation in pursuing the policy of "peaceful coexistence," that is, collaboration with imperialism, is fear of revolutionary upheavals elsewhere in the world. While neither center of bureaucratic power is averse to widening its influence and control, both of them stand in dread of disturbing the status quo because of the inevitable revolutionary domestic repercussions. That is why these conservatized rulers have quite consciously sought to collaborate with imperialism in maintaining the status quo. Tito is no different and no better.

The growth of political dissidence in the Soviet Union, as shown by mounting dissatisfaction among the intellectuals and broadening resistance among the oppressed nationalities, not to mention the "troubles" in Czechoslovakia in 1968 and Poland in 1970, heightened Moscow's eagerness for a deal with Nixon. In the case of China, the same predisposition to welcome any move by Nixon was increased by the pressures that came to the fore in the tumult of the "cultural revolution."

For both Peking and Moscow, the conflict in Vietnam represented a standing threat to internal stability in China and the Soviet Union, principally because of the example set by the Vietnamese masses in resisting the aggression and because of the widespread sympathy for them among the Chinese and Russian masses. In addition, there was the cost of sending material aid to the Vietnamese. While this was held to the minimum, it nonetheless represented an item in the budget that the bureaucratic caste begrudged expending.

To this should be added the bait of economic concessions held out by Nixon. The Soviet economy is under great strain because of bureaucratic mismanagement and the cost of trading in a world market dominated by capitalist cartels. It is now known that at the time of the secret negotiations for the detente, food was in short supply in the Soviet Union, not to mention many other shortages productive of unrest among the masses. Under the detente, Brezhnev-Kosygin were able to make huge grain purchases in the United States at a favorable price. It likewise became possible to secure other greatly needed items available in the United States. These purchases enabled the bureaucracy to ease immediate social pressures and to gain precious time, the better to handle domestic political opposition and to silence critical voices.

Beyond these immediate considerations, the detente opened the possibility of more far-reaching concessions to imperialism that, while temporarily strengthening the domestic position of the ruling bureaucratic castes, could undermine the planned economies of the Soviet Union and China. Concessions of this kind would include incursions of private capital, the security of which — along with the profits — would be guaranteed by the ruling bureaucrats. In the case of the Soviet Union, the projects being talked about run into the hundreds of millions and even billions of dollars. That, of course, is only to begin with.

Whether concessions on this order will be granted by

the Kremlin and by the Maoist regime remains to be seen. In the final analysis such concessions would constitute a giant threat to the economic base of the bureaucracy itself, that is, the planned economy on which it feeds in a parasitic way.

The domestic limitations to the detente are determined by the level of consciousness of the masses in the Soviet Union, who have given no signs of being prepared to give up the fundamental conquests of the October 1917 revolution, by the pressure this puts on the lower ranks of the bureaucracy, and by the ultimate instinct of self-preservation that may still exist in the top levels of the ruling caste.

That these limitations continue to play a role is shown by the insistence of the Kremlin that "peaceful coexistence" includes "peaceful competition" with capitalism internationally. This means that within the framework of collaboration in blocking and defeating revolutionary trends, Moscow and Peking intend to advance their own national-bureaucratic interests, however modestly and discreetly.

In an area like the Middle East, for example, Moscow has followed a consistent policy of maintaining a rather strong "presence" against the United States, supplying the Arab states with arms, some of them of much higher quality than were sent to Vietnam, for defense against the Israeli forces, which are supplied by Washington. Moscow's policy helps bolster the Arab capitalist states at the expense of revolutionary movements in the region, a line in complete conformity with the schema of "peaceful coexistence."

Moscow's pursuit of "peaceful competition" is not without its dialectical consequences. At the height of the October 1973 Middle East crisis, Nixon rattled the H-bomb, reminding the Kremlin and the world once again of the main logic governing the policies of U.S. imperialism.

The terms of the "cease-fire" in Vietnam sponsored by Peking and Moscow constituted one of the greatest of the many betrayals in the history of Stalinism. The two bureaucracies stabbed a workers state in the back while it was under ferocious assault by U.S. imperialism. They utilized their control of material supplies and their diplomatic and ideological influence over Hanoi and the National Liberation Front to compel acceptance of conditions highly detrimental to the military defense of the beleaguered workers state and to the advance of the Vietnamese revolution.

The fact that the Vietnamese leaders put the best face possible on the onerous conditions they felt they had to accept and that they even misrepresented a cease-fire imposed under these conditions as a great historic victory does not change the truth. Moscow and Peking, in forcing these conditions on the Vietnamese, committed a betrayal of major magnitude.

In previous decades, so great a betrayal would have been followed by demoralization and a period of stagnation in the world revolution. The general social turbulence on all continents today hardly permits the detente to serve as a long-lasting depressant in the period now opening.

Five convincing examples of this were the popular demonstrations that shook Thailand, Greece, and South Korea at the end of 1973, the militant strike of the coal miners in Britain that precipitated a national political crisis, and the twenty-four-hour general strike of three million industrial workers in Bombay and the state of Maharashtra in January 1974. The October war that broke out in the Arab East only nine months after the Vietnam cease-fire was signed served as another example of the difficulty of maintaining "peaceful coexistence."

In Vietnam itself, it can be added, civil strife continues to smolder, threatening to break out at any time on a much broader scale.

If the detente does gain time for imperialism, the colonial bourgeoisie, and the Stalinist bureaucracies, it can only end in social explosions of still greater force, and perhaps in totally unexpected areas. That time can be put to use in fostering the growth of Trotskyism so that the coming uprisings occur with leaderships on hand to guide them to a successful conclusion.

V. Maturing of the Subjective Conditions for Revolution

1. The Stage Reached by the Fourth International

From the preceding analysis of trends going back some years, it is evident that the objective conditions for the socialist revolution are ripe; they have even "begun to get somewhat rotten," as Trotsky put it thirty-five years ago. What has held the revolution from sweeping forward to a worldwide victory decades ago has been the unripeness of subjective conditions, which is expressed as a crisis in proletarian leadership. The degree of maturing of subjective conditions finds concrete measurement in the size and rate of expansion of the ranks of the Fourth International.

The class struggle has, of course, registered big ups and downs over the decades since 1938. Among the major victories can be listed the survival of the Soviet Union in World War II, the subsequent overturns of capitalism in Eastern Europe, the victory of the Chinese revolution and the resulting overturns of capitalism in North Korea and North Vietnam, and finally the victory of the Cuban revolution.

These developments greatly weakened world capitalism. However, capitalism still remains entrenched in the key industrial areas of North America, Western Europe, Japan, and important sectors of the colonial and semicolonial world; and world capitalism has become much more dangerous. The successes marked by the victory of the Soviet Union in World War II and the establishment of additional workers states did not bring forward a leadership capable of toppling capitalism in its main bastions. The distortion of the revolutionary pattern ascribable to the default of Stalinism blocked resolution of the crisis of proletarian leadership. In this sense, the situation outlined by Trotsky in 1938 has not been superseded.

To accurately analyze the prevailing objective situation is extremely important. Without a correct characterization of the conjunctural status of the class struggle, the Fourth International would quickly lose its way. We must know whether we face a downturn or an upturn. We must know what social sectors are in movement and whether they are developing in a favorable or unfavorable direction.

Just as important, however, is a correct characterization of the stage the Fourth International itself has reached. To determine that stage, an accurate analysis of the situation within the world Trotskyist movement is required.

In 1938, in projecting the strategic task facing the Fourth International, Leon Trotsky characterized the "next period" as "prerevolutionary," that is, a period of "agitation, propaganda and organization." In this period the sharpening contradictions of capitalism as a world system press the proletariat again and again toward reolutionary political action; the petty-bourgeois layers are repeatedly thrown into turmoil; the ruling classes are racked by periodic crises. Taking the world as a whole, these main features of a prerevolutionary situation will be seen again and again. Organization of a mass revolutionary party can turn these prerequisites into a "revolutionary" situation. Within this general framework, Trotsky outlined in an abstract and normative way the tasks that revolutionists should work out concretely in individual countries, which is where specific prerevolutionary situations with their particular characteristics occur.

Trotsky was not depreciating the period by calling it "prerevolutionary" instead of "revolutionary"; he was simply recognizing the reality, the better to change it. The fact was that in no country at that time had any Trotskyist party yet won a majority of the working class to its banners. Achievement of that task still lay ahead. Along with it, such tasks as arriving at dual power and actually engaging in and leading a showdown struggle for a government of the workers and their allies also remained in the future. To facilitate fulfilling these tasks, Trotsky proposed a Transitional Program, together with a method of keeping it up to date, which was adopted at the founding congress of the Fourth International.

The subjective conditions required for transcending the prerevolutionary period of agitation, propaganda and organization have not changed *qualitatively* since 1938. No party adhering to the Fourth International has as yet won a majority of the working class or of its militant vanguard. *The Fourth International still stands at the stage in which the primary task is the accumulation of cadres.*

As a consequence, actions undertaken by sections or groups of the Fourth International are directed at facilitating the accumulation of cadres. The *aim* of these actions is propagandistic.

Propagandistic actions have a single overall purpose — to help ripen the subjective conditions. On the most elementary level such actions include the educational work of discussions on the job, producing and circulating printed or duplicated material, conducting classes, forums, public meetings, engaging in electoral activities, etc. As the revolutionary Marxist forces grow and become rooted in the masses, the field of propagandistic actions broadens. In the process of winning leadership in a union or other mass organization, for instance, revolutionists participate in mobilizations of workers in strikes, demonstrations, defensive actions, etc., where they gain opportunities to demonstrate in practice the correctness of the program of revolutionary socialism and their capacities as proletarian leaders. The key objective at this stage, however, still remains that of accumulating cadres.

The quantitative development of the subjective side of the revolutionary process, as registered in the growth of the Trotskyist forces, makes it possible to exert an increasing influence in the class struggle. This may be registered in encouraging ways such as leadership in strike struggles or mass demonstrations. Nonetheless, on pain of losing that influence through a bad misstep, its limitations must be borne continually in mind. The Trotskyist influence in the class struggle today remains bound to developments in the objective situation completely beyond the control of our movement. To transcend this stage, to reach the position of being able to bring the objective situation under conscious control, that is, through negating bourgeois rule and establishing proletarian rule, requires *massive* forces — numbers so great as to make a qualitative difference. Once this qualitative point is reached, actions having an aim *qualitatively different* from those of the propaganda stage become both possible and necessary. The struggle for power, previously excluded, is placed on the agenda of the day.

It is vital to understand that characterizing the present stage as one of "agitation, propaganda and organization," that is, of revolutionary propaganda and assembling cadres, in no way implies that our activities are limited to commenting on events. Quite the reverse. As members of the proletariat, we participate in class-struggle actions to the utmost of our ability. To adopt any other course would signify falling into abstentionism, the mark of a sect, or substitutionism, the mark of an adventurist group.

To characterize the tasks faced by the Fourth International at its present stage as those of "agitation, propaganda and organization" does not arise from any lack of desire or will to move forward to the stage in which a mass revolutionary party has been built, a majority of the working class has been won, and the question of taking power is an immediate task. Nor does it arise from any lack of interest in the objective course of the class struggle, its ups and downs, and sudden or novel turns. The broad upsurges are of vital importance because they determine the appearance of prerevolutionary situations — sometimes in social explosions of the most unexpected nature as in Santo Domingo — which open the way for the swift expansion of the vanguard party and its being thrust forward into leadership of the working class, if it handles itself correctly as the Bolsheviks did.

The characterization of the present stage as one of "agitation, propaganda and organization" derives from an accurate appreciation of the actual number of cadres, the extent of their working-class roots, their ideological level, including hardness and immunity to alien class influences, their experience in practical organizational work, and their political capacities. A balance sheet of these items shows that the Fourth International is still weak, even in those countries where the Trotskyists have established a long record of stability and adherence to program and have made encouraging strides forward in the accumulation of cadres.

The maturity of objective conditions for the socialist revolution is matched qualitatively by the program of the Fourth International (which is brought up to date in correspondence with changes in objective conditions). It is the quantative side that requires concentrated attention in the immediate period ahead. What is required is multiplication of the forces adhering to the program of the Fourth International. At a certain point quantity will make a qualitative difference — in a country that has attained the prerevolutionary level, the subjective conditions will match the objective. The maturation of the party in size, training, and influence supplies the final component needed to make the situation revolutionary.

Clarity on this is absolutely essential. Confusion on such a decisive question as the relative size, influence, and power of the sections of the Fourth International means blocking the road to assembling the forces required for a socialist victory.

For instance, instead of concentrating on the task at hand — quantitative expansion — confusionists may decide to tinker with the program. Various groupings have tried that in the past only to leave the Trotskyist movement and disintegrate or, perhaps worse, simply vegetate.

Another line of experimentation is to seek to gain cadres by way of clever tricks. This nearly always boils down to sliding away from program to put on a more pleasing appearance in face of opposing currents.

Another variant is to count on something unexpected turning up in the objective development of the class struggle that will lighten, it not altogether do away with, the hard, day-in-day-out work of building a party — an ad hoc substitute for the party that will save everything at the last moment, thus permitting one in the meantime to live on hopes to a certain degree.

Still another variant is to look ahead to future possibilities, and, speculating on these, to apply tactics today that might be appropriate if and when these possibilities are realized. An extreme example is the initiation of "armed struggle" in situations where it can only be a caricature of the predictable course that a mass revolutionary party would adopt when the conquest of power is on the immediate agenda.

It cannot be stressed too emphatically that the primary task for the immediate period ahead is the *accumulation of cadres*. This can be accomplished through recruitment of individuals, through temporary blocs with other groups, or fusions. The possibility of fusions with other groups can grow in importance as the working-class upsurge continues, greatly speeding the accumulation of cadres and even lending tempestuous acceleration to the process of party building. These variants depend on concrete situations, including the political capacities of the leadership and the level of development of the rank and file of the sections of the Fourth International.

The axis of activities for the immediate period ahead must be decided on in the light of this reality. The framework of tasks is set by the frank and clear-sighted recognition that the central problems facing the Fourth International are those associated with the growth of small revolutionary propaganda organizations and not those faced by seasoned revolutionary parties of the masses about to take power.

Modest, realistic goals should be set. Success in achieving these can lead in a relatively short time in some countries to more ambitious targets. Winning cadres in this stage hinges on consistent *propaganda* advancing basic revolutionary-socialist themes in opposition to all other political currents, on appropriate and timely *agitation* around immediate, democratic, and transitional demands, and on efficient *organization*, particularly the development of professionals dedicated to advancing the revolutionary cause and committed to devoting all their time and energy to it.

Traps and pitfalls are not lacking. Inexperienced revolutionists can inadvertently cloud the political independence they really stand for by getting caught up in people's fronts that proclaim socialist aims. The well-meaning desire to find means of winning a hearing from the workers can lead to cutting corners on principles.

A snare of opposite nature in the last few years has been "minority violence." Under the misnomer "armed struggle," it has taken various forms such as guerrilla war, hijacking of planes, kidnappings, assassinations, and other "spectacular" actions carried out by small isolated groups. To engage in a premature armed confrontation with the capitalist state undoubtedly requires courage. However, it amounts to taking cadres required for political struggle and converting them into mere units on a military level where they are subject to quick liquidation by the vastly superior military forces of the capitalist state.

To call on small units to carry out a task requiring powers that can be supplied only by the masses is suicidal. To hope that the actions of such units will set off a social explosion constitutes ultraleft adventurism. The price of the error of substituting the "strategy of armed struggle" for the Leninist strategy of party building is loss of valuable cadres and serious, if not fatal, setbacks in the primary task facing a small group of revolutionists of becoming rooted in the masses.

In addition, a heavy price must be paid for the opportunist deviations from program that such mistakes encourage and foster. Instead of arming the masses militarily as hoped, the cadres themselves become disarmed politically. The case of the PRT-ERP in Argentina, which followed the guerrilla road until that road led it out of the Fourth International in 1973, is a signal warning.

The last world congress, it must now be acknowledged, took an incorrect position in relation to guerrilla warfare by adopting an orientation calling on the sections of the Fourth International in Latin America to prepare for and to engage in it as a strategic line.

The main task facing a small group of revolutionists, let it be repeated, is to recruit and train cadres. This holds true for all such groups whether they are in the imperialist sector, the colonial and semicolonial countries, or the bureaucratized workers states. The objective is to expand the group and its influence so that it gains the possibility of initiating mass actions. To accomplish this, the revolutionary cadres must be rooted in the trade unions or similar broad organizations of the working class. They bring revolutionary-Marxist ideas *into* the class struggle, doing this as *participants* and not as *outsiders*. In the day-to-day struggle they seek to prove the capacity of Trotskyists to correctly and courageously express the needs and interests of the masses, thereby gaining recognition as tested and dependable leaders completely devoted to the cause of the working class.

If cadres can be won directly in the key industries or in the most powerful organizations of the working class, this of course coincides directly with the main line of march, which is to mobilize the proletariat for the conquest of power. However, if recruiting possibilities are, for the moment, difficult in these sectors, but better in others, no principle of Bolshevism bars a temporary shift of attention. In such circumstances, the focus of work should be moved to peripheral industries or to peripheral unions. The key is to *link up with those social sectors that are in movement* and that offer the best opportunities for recruitment. A small group should not hesitate at following promising leads among oppressed nationalities, among radicalizing youth, male or female, on jobs, unemployed, or on the campus. An opponent political organization where a current happens to be developing in a revolutionary direction may offer promise of fresh forces. Dissident intellectuals (particularly in the bureaucratized workers states) may be a source of valuable cadres. The field of temporary concentration is a tactical matter — the aim is to *recruit, educate, assimilate.*

Publication of a journal should be undertaken as soon as possible. Assuming that the political line is correct and that articles are carefully written so that the particular audience where activity is being concentrated is drawn toward the journal, the main requisite is *regularity* of publication. Even if the journal is only mimeographed or handwritten (samizdat in the degenerated or deformed workers states; underground circulars in countries governed by military or fascist dictatorships), its regularity can be decisive in establishing its influence. Failure to produce a regular journal means stagnation. The Fourth International can cite dismal instances of this, in some cases involving sections in crucial situations — and not in the distant past (Bolivia, Chile).

Small revolutionary groups are often beset by problems that they find difficult to cope with because of inexperience. These include training cadres, developing a competent leadership, and functioning in accordance with Leninist norms. Solutions to such problems, which are always very concrete, can be facilitated by consultation with more seasoned sections of the Fourth International, a task that falls under the responsibility of the international center.

While everyone in the world Trotskyist movement is interested in how tactical questions are handled by the sections and sympathizing groups, a world congress cannot properly determine these, still less can it properly attempt to determine tactics for the Fourth International as a whole. To try to do otherwise inevitably leads to disorienting errors, a result anticipated by theory and confirmed by historical experience. The main purpose of a world congress is to draw balance sheets, project a political orientation, and determine the main axis of activities for the immediate period ahead.

2. Tasks of the Fourth International For the Period Immediately Ahead

With these provisos, certain broad areas of work can be indicated as meriting special attention by all sections and sympathizing groups of the Fourth International:

1. *Advancing class-struggle, left-wing formations in the trade unions in opposition to the conservative bureaucracies.* This is in line with the general proletarian orientation followed by the Fourth International since its foundation. In some countries, where the rise in working-class militancy has been most marked, new opportunities have opened up. The PST in Argentina and the Trotskyists in Spain have demonstrated how such situations can be turned to account in penetrating the industrial proletariat and furthering the growth of the Fourth International.

2. *Educational and organizational work among radicalizing students, apprentices, and youth in the factories.* Such work is greatly facilitated by an independent youth organization adhering to the program of Trotskyism but without the stress on complete dedication and firm discipline demanded of members of a revolutionary-Marxist party. For conjunctural reasons, such as the weakness

of the adult organization, some sections of the Fourth International have dissolved formerly affiliated youth organizations. Invariably this has raised new problems in developing young cadres and has hampered making maximum recruitment gains from the youth radicalization. Our movement as a whole should resume the goal it set for itself in its founding period — the creation of an independent international youth organization.

3. *Fraternal collaboration with national liberation organizations.* Productive work has been done in this field since the postwar rise of national liberation struggles, an outstanding example being the solidarity campaigns organized during the Algerian revolution. The new opportunities that have appeared in recent years in the imperialist countries for activities of this kind, like the collaboration with Malcolm X and with the Irish republicans, should be seized in an energetic way. The same holds true for the new opportunities that have appeared in connection with the struggle against national oppression in the bureaucratized workers states.

4. *Participation in peasant struggles.* In many countries such as Bolivia, Peru, India, Sri Lanka, etc., where the agrarian question remains unresolved, fresh upsurges of the peasantry are certain to occur, signs of this already being evident in some areas. Revolutionary Marxists should actively participate in these struggles from the beginning, attempting to give them revolutionary forms or organization and to link them up with the struggles of the proletariat in the cities. The value of work of this kind was demonstrated by the Peruvian section of the Fourth International in the early sixties. Hugo Blanco's leadership in the agrarian struggle in the Cuzco region still remains a model that can be profitably studied by Trotskyists wherever the peasantry constitutes a substantial sector of the population.

5. *Active support of the women's liberation movement.* The close attention paid by activists in the women's liberation movement to experiences in other countries plus their general willingness to consider revolutionary views with

an open mind have opened unusual opportunities for the participation of Trotskyists in this field and for international coordination of their activities. We should not wait for the women's liberation movement to develop by itself in countries where it is just beginning but should actively support it in the initial, formative stages when the considerable experience of the Trotskyist movement in organizing effective protests is most welcome, and when our opponents tend to be absent.

Besides work in these general areas, certain *internationally coordinated campaigns* can be projected, subject to modification in the light of events:

1. *In defense of the revolutionary struggles of oppressed peoples.* A good example in the past period was the international campaign in defense of the Vietnamese revolution. Another was the campaign in defense of the Palestinian revolution.

Comparable campaigns in the coming period should be waged in behalf of the Irish freedom struggle, the efforts of the Portuguese colonies to achieve national independence, and similar anti-imperialist struggles elsewhere.

The struggles of national minorities in the bureaucratized workers states should be handled in the same way.

Such work enhances the possibility for recruiting and developing Trotskyist cadres from among the many students and workers of these oppressed nations who are temporarily resident in Europe and North America where established Trotskyist organizations already exist. The nuclei of new sections can be built in part through this work, as experience has shown.

2. *In defense of political prisoners in all lands.* Specific campaigns like the one for political prisoners in Argentina in the past period can be waged for other areas, the ones most prominent at the moment being Chile, Brazil, the Soviet Union, Ireland, Spain, Iran, South Vietnam, Uruguay, and China.

3. *In defense of sections and leaders of the Fourth International hit by repressive measures.* The outstanding model for such campaigns was the one conducted to save the life of Hugo Blanco. The case of Luis Vitale is on the current agenda. In totalitarian Spain, the Trotskyist movement has been hit by dozens of arrests. The fight